This book has been updated
five times. This edition was
revised in February 1972.

Printed in Great Britain
at the Shenval Press
London and Harlow

a Consumer Publication

WHAT TO DO WHEN SOMEONE DIES

Consumers' Association
publishers of **Which?**
14 Buckingham Street
London WC2N 6DS

a Consumer Publication

edited by   Edith Rudinger

published by   Consumers' Association
publishers of **Which?**

Consumer publications are
available from Consumers'
Association, or through
booksellers. Details of
other Consumer Publications
are given at the end of
this book.

CONTENTS

Foreword

Death, and the formalities   *page* 9

– *Scotland*   31

Disposal   37

– burial   42

– cremation   49

The funeral   59

– *Scotland*   88

What else has to be done   90

Grants, allowances and pensions   95

Index   108

The book deals with the formalities and procedure in England and Wales; the important differences which apply in Scotland are given on pages 31–36 and on pages 88–89.

This book aims to help those who have never had to deal with the arrangements that must be made after a death – getting a doctor's certificate and registering, deciding whether to bury or cremate, choosing an undertaker and a coffin, putting notices in the papers, selecting the form of service, claiming national insurance benefits. It explains the function of people with whom they will come in contact, often for the first time. They will get help and guidance from the doctor, the registrar, the undertaker, the clergyman, the cemetery or crematorium officials, the Department of Health and Social Security and, in some circumstances, the police and the coroner. However, it is the executor or nearest relative who has to make the decisions, often at a time of personal distress or harassment, and *What to do when someone dies* describes what needs to be done, when, and how to set about it.

No attempt is made to deal with the personal or social aspects of death, such as the psychology of grief and shock or the conventions of mourning, nor does it trace the historical development of rituals and of attitudes to death.

You may discover someone apparently dead, and it can be difficult to tell whether he really is dead or not. For instance, someone rescued from water may appear not to breathe, yet might be revived by artificial respiration.

The body temperature drops at the rate of two to three degrees Fahrenheit an hour for the first few hours after death, so someone who has been dead for an hour or so is appreciably colder than normal. The extremities – feet and hands – get cold first. But very low body temperature alone is not a sure sign of death because comatose or unconscious people can also seem abnormally cold.

Telling the doctor
If there is any doubt whether someone is dead, treat him as being still alive. The first thing to do is to call the doctor. If you do not know how or where to get hold of a doctor, ring the telephone operator and ask for the name and number of a local doctor from the list of doctors kept by the telephone exchange.

Even if it seems certain that the person really is dead, you should let his doctor know soon. But if the doctor had been in attendance and the death was not unexpected, there may be no need to telephone him in the middle of the night instead of waiting until the next morning. Ask whether the doctor is going to come. If the death was peaceful and expected, the doctor may not feel it necessary to see the body, or may not come straightaway. Some doctors make it a practice to see the body of every patient who has died.

You should tell the doctor if the body is to be cremated because if so the doctor will have to examine the body and arrange for another doctor to do so, too. If the body is not to be cremated, you can ask an undertaker to come straightaway to take the body away or to lay it out; he may charge for this service.

Laying out the body

Rigor mortis, a stiffening of the muscles, usually begins within about 6 hours after death, and gradually extends over the whole body in about 18 hours, after which it begins to wear off. Rigor mortis is less pronounced in the body of an old person. When someone has been dead for about half an hour or more, parts of the skin will have started to discolour. This discoloration, which is called post mortem staining, is caused by the blood sinking under the action of gravity.

Laying out, usually done by a nurse or by one of the undertaker's staff, should be done as soon as possible. The body is washed, the natural orifices stopped up with cotton wool and a napkin, and clean clothes put on. The eyelids are closed and the jaw supported, the hair is tidied and the arms and feet put straight. A man may need to be shaved. When the laying out is done at home, the person laying out usually brings most of the necessary equipment, but may ask to be given a sheet and some towels, a pillow, warm water, soap and disinfectant, and perhaps a nightdress or pyjamas or a shirt to put on the body.

If someone has died quietly and expectedly at home and in bed it is all right to tidy the room and rearrange or lay out the body. But if you discover a dead body in any other circumstances, do as little as possible to it until the doctor comes. Do not move it unless it is likely to be damaged or cause damage where it is.

Calling the police

If you think that death appears to have been caused by an accident or violence, or to have occurred in other suspicious circumstances, you should at once inform the police. Do not touch or move anything in the room, nor allow anyone else to do so, until the police say that you may. The police will almost certainly want to take statements from anyone who was with the deceased when he died, or who discovered the body, but no one is obliged to give a statement to the police. If there is an inquest later, anyone who has made a statement is liable to be called as a witness. If a body cannot be immediately identified, the police circulate a description in police journals, and occasionally to the general press, too. Anyone who might be able to identify the body usually has to go to the mortuary with the police to do so.

If the police are called and no relative or other person responsible is immediately available, the police take possession of any cash or valuables. As a general rule, this property is given up to whoever can later prove his right to it. The police also take away any article which may have a bearing on the cause of death – a letter or bottle of pills, for example – in case this is needed by the coroner.

Medical certificate of cause of death

The law requires that every death in this country shall be registered. For this, medical evidence of the cause of death must be given. The person who has authority to do so is either the coroner or, more usually, the doctor who was looking after the deceased during the final illness. The doctor is legally bound to issue a medical certificate of cause of death, even in cases when he is not certain of the precise cause. On the medical certificate he states to the best of his knowledge and belief the cause of death, the last date on which the doctor had seen the deceased alive, and whether or not a doctor has seen the body. The doctor is not allowed to charge for this certificate.

The doctor either gives the certificate to one of the deceased's relatives to take to the registrar of the area in which the death took place or he sends it to the registrar by post. On the back of the certificate the doctor indicates if he has reported the case to the coroner.

When a death has been reported to the coroner, the registrar cannot register the death until the coroner authorises him to do so.

The coroner

The office of the coroner was instituted in England in norman times. He was the king's officer appointed for a shire or a borough for the purpose of keeping an eye on the sheriff, keeping a record of all sudden deaths (that is, deaths which were 'against the course of nature') and of any occurrence by which monies or property might be forfeit and revert to the crown.

Nowadays the coroner is a qualified doctor or lawyer, some-times both. He is appointed by the county or county borough council but is responsible to no one except the crown. Some of his duties are now largely archaic, such as instituting in-quiries regarding the finding of any gold or silver whose ownership is unknown, in order to discover whether it is treasure trove and therefore belongs to the crown. His main function is to investigate any death which has been reported to him.

A death has to be reported to the coroner if the doctor had not attended the deceased at all during his last illness. Even if the doctor had been treating him, if he had not seen him within the last 14 days, the death will have to be reported to the coroner unless the doctor comes to see the body. (In Northern Ireland, the period within which the doctor should have last seen the patient is 28 days.)

Any death that was sudden must be reported to the coroner; also a death caused either directly or indirectly by any kind of accident, if the circumstances of the death are in any way suspicious (such as violence or neglect), and if the medical cause is unknown.

The coroner must be notified of any death which takes place during an operation, and if death follows an operation required after an injury. Suicides, and deaths which may have been caused by an abortion, by drugs, alcoholism, or by poisoning (including food poisoning) must be reported. So must a death attributable to what is classified as an industrial disease, and in some cases one caused or accelerated by an injury received during military service.

Generally, it is the doctor who reports a death to the coroner, or the police. The registrar of births and deaths will do so if the cause or circumstances of the death warrant it. But anyone who is uneasy about the apparent cause of a death has the right to inform the coroner for the district. By telephoning a police station you can find out who the coroner for the relevant district is and how to get in touch with him. This is usually through the coroner's officer, who is almost always a police officer. There may be some circumstances which you feel are contributory to the death but may not be known to the doctor – such as an old war wound or injury – which can be established by a post mortem examination.

Reporting a death to the coroner does not inevitably mean a post mortem or an inquest, although the majority of deaths reported to a coroner do lead to a post mortem; about one-fifth lead to an inquest. These proportions vary from district to district because it is up to each individual coroner to decide what action shall be taken.

If, after considering the circumstances of a death, the coroner decides that there is no need for further investigation, he sends a formal notice of his decision to the registrar of the district. If the registrar knows who the next of kin are he gets in touch with them and tells them that he is now in a position to register the death. If the death had been reported to the coroner direct, the registrar will not know who the next of kin are, so he has to wait until someone comes to him.

Post mortem

If the coroner orders a post mortem, no one can appeal against his decision. The coroner's officer becomes responsible for the body, and has it removed to the mortuary if it is not already there.

A post mortem is usually needed to establish with certainty the medical cause of death. It may be important to be able to state the medical cause of death accurately if there are any legal proceedings arising from the death.

If the post mortem should reveal that the death was due to a natural cause and no other circumstances warrant further investigation, the coroner notifies the registrar. The coroner has no duty to inform the next of kin of the result of the post mortem. In some districts, the coroner's officer or another policeman calls on the family to tell them; otherwise the next of kin have to enquire at the registrar's office every few days to find out whether the coroner's notification has arrived, or get the undertaker to find out.

After the post mortem the body becomes again the responsibility of the family, unless there is to be an inquest.

Inquest

The coroner can choose to hold an inquest on any death reported to him. But if he has reasonable grounds for suspecting that the death was violent or unnatural, he is legally obliged to hold an inquest. He is also obliged to hold one when a person has died in circumstances where the law requires an inquest to be held – for example, in prison or following a motoring accident.

An inquest is held to establish who the deceased was, how, when and where he died, and any other particulars required for the registration of the death. If the inquest reveals that the death was caused by murder, manslaughter or infanticide, the court may say who is to be charged. If, in the meantime, the police have charged someone, the inquest is adjourned to await the result of the proceedings, and is not usually resumed.

Inquests are formal proceedings to which the public are generally admitted. To find out when and where an inquest is being held, ask at the police station nearest the place of death or telephone the local coroner's office.

A coroner's court is a court of law, even though no one is accused. Witnesses are on oath. The coroner can admit any evidence, including, if he sees fit, hearsay evidence which in other courts of law might be inadmissible. The coroner will call as witnesses some of the people who made statements to the police about the death. A policeman will have gone round beforehand to tell witnesses the date, place and time of the inquest. If anyone who has been requested to come as a witness says that he will not attend the inquest, he will be officially instructed by the coroner to do so and a coroner's summons can be served to make sure the witness will come. Witnesses can claim from the court their expenses and compensation for loss of time.

There is a minimum amount of pomp and ceremony at an inquest. The coroner calls witnesses in turn from the main part of the court to come up to the witness box. Each witness swears or affirms that he 'will speak the truth, the whole truth and nothing but the truth'. The taking of the oath is the only formal element in the proceedings.

First the coroner questions the witness, then, with his permission, the witness can be examined by anyone present who has a legal interest in the case (or by that person's legal representative). You have such an interest, for instance, if the person who was killed was a close relative, but not if you are the secretary of the Society for the Abolition of Road Traffic and want to speak in the case of a motor accident. When all the witnesses have been heard, the coroner sums up. If you know you will want to give evidence or examine a witness, tell the coroner's officer beforehand, so that the coroner can call you at the right moment. You should speak before the coroner has summed up.

There should be no expense to the family arising out of the inquest, unless the services of a solicitor are needed. Many people think it wise for the family to be represented by a solicitor in cases of death resulting from an accident or occupational disease, as there may be compensation claims to be made later and a solicitor would be better able to make use of the evidence presented at an inquest.

If there is reason to suspect that the death was due to murder, manslaughter or infanticide, or to a motoring, rail or air accident, the coroner must hold an inquest with a jury. A jury is also required for an inquest after the death of a prisoner, or a death resulting from accidents in certain occupations (such as mining) or industrial diseases. In all other cases, an inquest is held with or without a jury, according to the coroner's decision.

The jury for an inquest consists of not less than seven and not more than eleven men or women from the current list of voters eligible for jury service. The jurors are on oath. Although the coroner must view the body, the jury need not unless the coroner directs them to.

At the end of his summing up the coroner directs the jury as to the law and the possible verdicts they may bring in. A majority verdict is acceptable, provided that the minority is not more than two. Each member tells the foreman what he thinks and the foreman tells the coroner their joint verdict. The jury do not usually leave the court to discuss their decision but may do so. If there is no jury, the coroner gives his verdict at the end of his summing up of the case.

Sometimes the coroner opens an inquest merely in order to establish the identity of the deceased, and then immediately adjourns it, so that further investigations can take place. The reason for having such a brief inquest is for the coroner to be able to give his authority for the body to be buried or cremated. After this inquest, the coroner gives or sends to the next of kin or other responsible person, a certificate-for-cremation or an order for burial, whichever is required.

When an inquest is completed, the coroner sends a certificate-after-inquest to the registrar of births and deaths of the district in which the death took place or in which the body was found. This certificate provides the registrar with the information he requires to register the death.

Registering

If there has been an inquest, the details in the coroner's certificate-after-inquest are all the registrar needs. In all other cases, someone has to give him the information necessary for registering the death, and has to sign the register. In this country all deaths should be registered within five days of death. Registration can be delayed for a further nine days provided the registrar receives, in writing, the particulars to be registered, including medical evidence of the cause of death.

Under english law all deaths must be registered in the sub-district in which they took place or in which the body was found. A list of names, addresses and telephone numbers of local registrars is usually displayed in doctors' surgeries, in post offices, and in public libraries and other public buildings, together with their office hours and a description of the sub-district they cover.

Usually, whoever is giving the information goes in person to the registrar's office. Very few registration districts have an appointment system; normally you just go along during the registrar's office hours and wait until he is free to see you.

The law defines who qualifies to give the required information to the registrar. If the death occurred in a house or inside any other building the informant can be either a relative who was there at the death or during the last illness, or a relative who lives, or happens to be, in the sub-district of the registrar for the deceased. If there is no eligible relative, the informant may be any other person who was present at the death; the head of the household (in a public institution the senior resident officer); anyone else living in the house who knew about the death; or the person responsible for making the funeral arrangements, or in charge of the body (this will be the police if the body cannot be identified).

If the person had been found dead out of doors, the informant could be a relative who has enough information about the deceased to complete the details for the registrar; anyone who happened to be there when the person died or who found the body; or whoever is responsible for making the funeral arrangements.

In England a 'notice to informant' is attached to the doctor's medical certificate of cause of death. On the back is the list of people who can act as informants. The responsibility of being an informant must not be delegated to anyone not qualified to act. The doctor should give the notice to the person who is going to be the informant, and the informant should take it to the registrar. If he does not have the medical evidence of the cause of death (because the doctor is posting the medical certificate direct to the registrar), the informant should allow time for the evidence to reach the registrar before he goes to register the death. If, when he gets the evidence, the registrar finds that the information the doctor has been able to give on the medical certificate of cause of death is inadequate, he will have to report the death to the coroner. He will also do so if it turns out that the death was due to some cause, such as an old war wound, which makes it reportable.

The procedure for registering a death is a simple question-and-answer interview between the registrar and the informant. The registrar will, first of all, make sure that the death took place in his sub-district; he cannot register a death which occurred in any place outside his jurisdiction. He will ask in what capacity whoever is registering the death qualifies to be the informant – relative, present at the death, or other reason.

He then fills in a draft form for the register of deaths with details of the informant, the date of death and exactly where it occurred, the name and surname of the dead person. It is as well to give all the names by which the deceased had ever been known, so that there can be no doubt who the particulars refer to. In order to avoid difficulties over identity in connection with probate, insurance policies, pensions and bank accounts, the names should be the same as those on birth and marriage certificates, and on any other relevant documents. The maiden surname of a married woman is required. The sex of the dead person, date and place of birth, and address are entered. If he died away from home, his home address should be given.

Next, the registrar will ask what was the last full-time occupation of the deceased, and whether he or she was retired at the time of death. The description of the occupation should be precise: 'miner' could be anyone from a geologist prospecting for diamond-bearing rock strata in the african veldt to a colliery pithead baths attendant.

The occupation of a woman who was married or widowed

at the time of her death is recorded, and in addition to this and irrespective of her own occupation or profession, she would be described as 'wife of' or 'widow of' followed by the name and occupation of her husband.

A woman over sixteen who had never been married or a woman whose marriage had been dissolved would have her occupation described, with no reference to her marital status.

Children under the age of fifteen are described as 'son of' or 'daughter of', followed by the name and occupation of the father. If the child was illegitimate and paternity had not been established, the name of the mother is entered. For an adopted child, the description 'adopted son of' or 'adopted daughter of' could be used, if the informant prefers.

The registrar copies the medical cause of death from the doctor's certificate or the coroner's notification, and adds the name and qualification of the doctor or coroner.

On the draft form, but not in the register itself, the registrar enters the deceased's national health service number or his date of birth. If the deceased was over sixteen years old, additional information is requested: marital status at the time of death (single, married, widowed or divorced) and the age of any widow or widower left. This information is not entered in the register in England and Wales, and is used only for the preparation of population statistics by the registrar general.

The informant should check the draft of the proposed entry in the register to make sure that there is nothing wrong or misleading in it. When the particulars are agreed, the registrar makes the entry in the register itself and asks the informant to check and sign it. The informant should sign his usual signature, even if this is not his whole name. The registrar has to use special ink for the register, so sign with the pen he offers.

After adding the date of the registration, the registrar himself signs the entry in the final space. Any errors can be corrected without formality before the entry has been signed, but once it is signed by the registrar, the entry cannot be corrected without the authority of the registrar general, who may require documentary evidence to justify the correction.

FOR REGISTRATION – THE DOCUMENTS

notice to informant	from doctor	gives details of who must register death and what particulars will be required	via relative to registrar
medical certificate of cause of death	from doctor	states cause of death	to registrar (direct or via relative)
if coroner involved: coroner's notification	from coroner	confirms or gives details of cause of death	direct to registrar
or			
coroner's certificate-after-inquest	from coroner	gives all the particulars required for death to be registered	direct to registrar

The registrar can now let you have copies of the entry in the register (the death certificates) which you may need for probate and other purposes.

Make a note of the number of the entry in the register and the date, and of the registration district, because you may need more copies of the entry later.

At the time of registering the death, the registrar will ask for the deceased's medical card. If the informant has not brought it, the registrar will give him a stamped addressed envelope to send it later. This is to enable the national health service register to be kept up to date. Any order book for a pension or allowance based on war service must be handed to the registrar who will forward it to the authority who had issued it. You should make a note of the pension or allowance number (not the number of the particular book) before handing over the book.

Death certificates
In order to claim various payments from the state after someone has died, a certificate which confirms the registration of the death is needed. When registering the death, the registrar issues this free. This certificate is of use only when claiming national insurance benefits. The application form for claiming (the Department of Health and Social Security's form B.D.8) is printed on the back of the certificate. If registration of the death has had to be delayed for any reason, the registrar amends the certificate of registration to a certificate of notification of death, provided he has received the necessary evidence of death from the doctor or coroner. If the delay is due to an inquest being held, and the next of kin need to claim any payments or benefits straightaway, they can ask the coroner for a written statement to use in place of a death certificate.

The other certificates you will need when making arrangements about the deceased's affairs are all certified copies of the entry of death in the register. There is no shortened form as in the case of birth certificates. A 'standard' death certificate has to accompany an application for a grant of probate or letters of administration. It costs 25p in England and Wales (22½p in Northern Ireland).

For claiming from a registered friendly society, either the standard 25p death certificate can be used or another certificate costing 10p. To obtain this certificate you must tell the registrar the name of the friendly society concerned.

You may not know from the name of the society or company

whether it is an industrial assurance company or friendly society, but if you take the policies or a list of the full titles with you to the registrar, he should be able to tell you.

Neither the standard certificate nor the friendly society certificate can be accepted for claims in connection with insurance taken out on the life of the parent or grandparent by a child, adopted child, stepchild or grandchild. A 'special' certificate costing 10p must be obtained for this.

On the application form for this certificate the applicant certifies that he had taken out an insurance on the life of the deceased parent or grandparent and states his relationship. Unlike other death certificates it is solely for the use of the applicant, whose name and address is given. Only one of these special death certificates is issued to any one person. If more than one insurance company is involved, the certificate should be reclaimed after each company has endorsed it. If the original certificate is lost or destroyed, a duplicate can only be obtained if the applicant makes a statutory declaration in front of a JP, magistrate or commissioner for oaths.

Yet another form of death certificate, also costing 10p, is issued for 'certain other statutory purposes' – for claiming under the Family Allowances Act, National Insurance Act or National Insurance (Industrial Injuries) Act; and, in cases where probate is not required, for encashing national savings certificates, post office or trustee savings bank deposits or premium savings bonds. If the free certificate of registration of the death (incorporating form B.D.8) has been lost or destroyed, this death certificate can be used instead.

Nearly all insurance companies regard the production of a death certificate of one form or another as part of the claim against them.

If you want the registrar to advise you about the number and type of certificates you may need, take with you a list of the various purposes for which you think some evidence of the death may be required. You can get a further supply of certificates if any come to be needed later on.

DEATH CERTIFICATES

certificate of registration/ notification of death (incorporating form B.D.8)	free	for claiming death grant and widow's benefit from the Department of Health and Social Security
standard death certificate	25p (22½p in N.I.)	for obtaining probate; for private claims such as life insurance and pension schemes; also for friendly societies
special death certificate	10p	for claiming insurance taken out on the life of a parent or grandparent
certificate for purposes of Friendly Societies Acts	10p	for claiming from a registered friendly society
certificate for certain statutory purposes	10p	for claiming on trustee savings banks, national savings banks, national savings certificates and premium savings bonds, when probate is not required; also for claiming under National Insurance Act and Family Allowances Act if the certificate of registration/notification of death has been lost or destroyed, and for claiming under the National Insurance (Industrial Injuries) Act

If you need a standard death certificate later on, the certificate will cost you 40p. If the death was fairly recent, you apply to the registrar who registered it. If the death was registered more than about a year previously, standard death certificates can be obtained from the General Register Office, Somerset House, London WC2R 1LR. The charge is 40p if you go in person to Somerset House; 65p if you apply by post.

In Northern Ireland, the General Register Office address is Fermanagh House, Ormeau Avenue, Belfast BT2 8HX, and the charge for a standard death certificate is 22½p, with a search fee of 10p in addition.

If you need to apply for certificates from the registrar of another district, your local registrar can tell you the names and addresses of all other registrars. He can give you the application forms needed for the various certificates and help you to complete them. With any postal application for a certificate, you must send the necessary cheque or postal order and a stamped addressed envelope. When you get certificates from your local registrar in person, you are expected to pay there and then.

Death in hospital

If death has taken place in a hospital or similar institution, what happens up to the time of registering is slightly different from the arrangements that have to be made when the death was at home.

The next of kin are informed by the ward sister. If death was unexpected, or the result of an accident, it may be the police who find and tell the next of kin. A member of the family is asked to come to the hospital and, if the dead person was not already a patient in the hospital, may have to identify the body, usually not in the mortuary but by being shown the body in another room. Hospitals differ from each other in procedure but it is usually the administrative rather than the medical staff who make the arrangements with the relatives; in some hospitals it is one of the head porter's duties, in others the relatives may have to deal with several people. Whoever goes to the hospital may be asked to take away the deceased's possessions, so it is as well to take along a suitcase. A shroud will be provided under the national health service, if required.

Hospitals often want to carry out a post mortem examination to find out more about the cause of death. The hospital cannot carry out such a post mortem without the permission of the deceased's next of kin. The person who goes to the hospital following a death should therefore be prepared to say whether the next of kin will allow the hospital to carry out a post mortem, and, if so, to sign a consent form. Relatives are told the result of the post mortem, if they want to know.

The medical certificate of cause of death is usually completed by the hospital doctor, and if the body is to be cremated, the hospital will arrange for the necessary medical forms to be completed. However, if the person had died before a hospital doctor had a chance to diagnose the case, the dead person's own doctor is asked to issue the medical certificate. If he cannot, the hospital will report the death to the coroner. A hospital will also report to the coroner a death that took place when the patient was undergoing an operation, or was under the effects of an anaesthetic, or in any other circumstances which have to be reported. The responsibility for the body is then transferred from the hospital to the coroner, and the coroner's office not the hospital is where the relatives should then seek information.

If the certificate of cause of death can be issued at the hospital and the death is not being reported to the coroner, the body is kept in the hospital mortuary until the family arranges for it to be taken away. The procedure for registering the death is the same as for an ordinary death at home, but the registration must be done at the office of the registrar in whose district the hospital is.

Stillbirths

The process of registering a stillbirth is a mixture of registering a birth and registering a death and has to be done within 42 days. People qualified to register a stillbirth (as for live births) are the mother; the father, if the child would have been legitimate had it been born alive; the occupier of the house or other premises in which the stillbirth occurred; a person who was present at the stillbirth or who found the stillborn child.

A stillborn child is a child born after the 28th week of pregnancy which did not at any time breathe or show any other signs of life. Foetal death before the 28th week does not fall within the legal definition of a stillbirth and is usually considered a miscarriage.

If a doctor was in attendance at a stillbirth or examined the body of the stillborn child, he gives a certificate of stillbirth, stating the cause of death and the duration of the pregnancy. A certified midwife can issue the certificate if no doctor was there. If no doctor or midwife was in attendance at, or after, the birth, one of the parents, or someone who was in the house at the time, can make a declaration on a form (form 35, available from the registrar of births and deaths), saying that to the best of his or her knowledge and belief the child was stillborn. If there is any doubt whether the child was born alive or not, the case must be reported to the coroner of the district, who may then order a post mortem or an inquest and will issue a certificate of the cause of death when he has completed his inquiries.

When registering a stillbirth, the registrar has to have the doctor's or midwife's certificate, or a declaration of the stillbirth. Whoever goes to register has to tell the registrar the name, surname and occupation of the father (if the child would have been legitimate), and his place of birth. The name, surname and maiden surname of the mother, her place of birth and her usual residence at the time of the child's birth are required, and if she had never been married, also her occupation. If the father and mother are married to each other, the registrar asks the month and year of the marriage, and the number of the mother's previous children, both born alive and stillborn, by her present and any former husband; this information is needed for statistical purposes only in order to forecast population trends.

Disposal certificate

Once a death has been registered, the registrar can issue a certificate, referred to generally as the disposal certificate, authorising either burial or application for cremation. A body cannot be buried or cremated without this certificate or its equivalent, namely the coroner's order for burial or certificate-for-cremation. It is unwise to make more than provisional arrangements for the funeral until you have a certificate for disposal.

You will get authority to dispose of the body from the registrar or from the coroner but not from both. If the death has been reported to the coroner, only he can give a certificate authorising cremation.

After an inquest, the coroner can issue an order for burial or a certificate-for-cremation. After a post mortem which is not being followed by an inquest, the coroner can issue a certificate-for-cremation; however, if the body is to be buried, it is the registrar who has to issue the disposal certificate.

No fees are charged for a disposal certificate. If you lose it, you or the burial or crematorium officials have to apply to the registrar or the coroner who issued the original certificate for a duplicate. There is no charge for this duplicate.

Once you have obtained a certificate for disposal from the registrar or the coroner, give it to the undertaker or take it direct to the church, cemetery or crematorium officials. Without it they will not bury or cremate a body. It is the responsibility of the church, cemetery or crematorium to complete part C of the disposal certificate and to return it to the registrar. If the registrar does not receive it within 14 days of the certificate having been issued, he will get in touch with the person to whom the disposal certificate had been given to find out what is happening. If a further 14 days elapse without a satisfactory reply, the registrar reports the facts to the medical officer of health for the district who will investigate the case. He may then, if circumstances warrant, take out a court order so that he can remove the body and dispose of it.

The registrar can issue a disposal certificate before registering a death but only when he has already received the requisite information (including medical evidence) and is just waiting for the informant to come and sign the register. This may arise, for instance, when the only suitable informant is ill in hospital but the funeral has to take place. A disposal certificate issued by the registrar before registration authorises burial only; cremation authorities do not accept such a certificate.

Medical certificate of cause of death

The medical certificate of cause of death given by doctors in Scotland is similar to that in England. The obligation to give the certificate rests on the doctor who attended the deceased during his last illness but, if there was no doctor in attendance, the certificate may be issued by any doctor who is able to do so. The doctor hands the certificate to a relative to take to the local registrar or sends it direct to the registrar. In the majority of cases, the certificate is issued to a relative. This certificate does not incorporate a notice to informant, nor does it contain the list of the people who can act as informant.

If a medical certificate of cause of death cannot be given, the registrar can, nevertheless, register the death but must report the facts of the case to the procurator fiscal.

The procurator fiscal

There are no coroners in Scotland and the duties which in England would be carried out by a coroner are in Scotland carried out by a procurator fiscal. The procurator fiscal is a full-time law officer, who comes under the Lord Advocate.

The procurator fiscal has many functions, including responsibility for investigating all unexpected and violent deaths and also any death which occurred under suspicious circumstances. If he is satisfied with the doctor's medical certificate and any evidence he receives from the police, he need take no further action. If, however, the procurator fiscal considers a further medical report is necessary, he requests a medical practitioner (frequently a police surgeon) to report to him 'on soul and conscience' what he considers was the cause of death. In the majority of cases, a post mortem is not carried out and the doctor certifies the cause of death after an external examination. The mere fact that the cause of death is in a medical sense unexplained is not a ground for ordering a dissection at the public expense, provided the intrinsic circumstances sufficiently explain the cause of death in a popular sense and do not raise a suspicion of criminality or negligence. In cases where the procurator fiscal decides a post mortem is necessary, permission to carry it out is given by the sheriff. One doctor is usually sufficient but if, while conducting the dissection, the doctor finds unexpected difficulties, the procurator fiscal may decide to bring in a second doctor in order to be able to certify the cause of death. In all cases where there is a possibility of criminal proceedings being taken against someone and it is necessary to prove the fact and cause of death, a post mortem should be carried out by two medical practitioners.

Deaths in prison and as the result of an accident during work must be the subject of a public inquiry, which takes the place of an inquest in England. If a person has died of natural causes while engaged in industrial employment or occupation, there may, but will not necessarily, be a public inquiry.

Unlike in England where a coroner himself decides what he shall or shall not do, in Scotland the procurator fiscal reports certain cases to the crown office and it is the Lord Advocate who makes the final decision about whether a public inquiry is to be held. In all other cases, investigations made into sudden deaths are carried out by the procurator fiscal confidentially.

Before reporting a case to the crown office, unless there is a likelihood of criminal proceedings being taken, the procurator fiscal interviews witnesses and the relatives in private (this is called a precognition).

Cases which are reported to the crown office because they may result in a public inquiry are deaths following a road accident or otherwise directly or indirectly connected with the action of a third party, and where there is an issue of public interest at stake – for instance, to prevent a recurrence of similar circumstances.

Whereas at an inquest in England the coroner interviews the witnesses and does the summing up of the case, a public inquiry in Scotland is heard before the sheriff and a jury of seven in the local *sheriff court. The procurator fiscal examines the witnesses but it is the sheriff who sums up and receives the jury's verdict.*

When he has completed his investigations, the procurator fiscal notifies the result of his findings to the registrar general. If the death has already been registered, the registrar general lets the local registrar know if any changes need to be made to the entry. If the death has not already been registered, the procurator fiscal sends a note of his findings to the registrar of the district in which the death occurred, together with the name and address of a relative or friend who can act as informant.

Registering
In Scotland, the law requires that every death must be registered within 8 days from the date of death.

The person qualified to act as informant for registering a death is any relative of the deceased, any person present at the death, the deceased's executor or other legal representative, the occupier of the premises where the death took place, or any person having knowledge of the particulars to be registered.

While in England a death must be registered in the registration office for the district in which the death occurred, in Scotland the death may be registered in the office for the district in which the death occurred or in the office for the district in which the deceased had normally resided before his death, provided this was also in Scotland. Deaths of visitors to Scotland must be registered where the death took place.

As in England, the procedure for registering a death is a simple question-and-answer interview between registrar and informant. The registrar will demand the production of a medical certificate of cause of death or, failing that, the name and address of a doctor who can be asked to give the certificate. The information required by a scottish registrar to register a death is much the same as in England and Wales, except that he also needs to know the time of death, if the deceased was married the name and occupation of the surviving spouse, the name and occupation of the deceased's father and the name and maiden surname of the mother, and whether the parents are alive or dead.

When the form of particulars has been completed, the registrar asks the informant to read it over carefully to ensure that all the particulars are correct, and to sign it. The registrar then makes the entry in the register and asks the informant to check it carefully and sign the entry. The registrar completes the entry by adding the date of registration and his own signature.

Stillbirths

A stillbirth in Scotland must be registered within 21 days. As in England, if no doctor or midwife can issue a certificate of still-birth, an informant must make a declaration on a special form. In Scotland this is form 7, obtainable from the registrar. All such cases, and any case where there is doubt as to whether the child was born alive or not, are reported to the procurator fiscal who issues a certificate of cause of death after he has completed his investigations.

If the body is to be cremated, a certificate of stillbirth must be given by the doctor who was in attendance at the confinement (or who conducted a post mortem). The stillbirth must have been registered before cremation can take place.

A stillbirth can be registered either in the district in which it took place or in the district in which the mother of the stillborn child was ordinarily resident at the time of the stillbirth.

The informant must produce to the registrar a doctor's or midwife's certificate, or the completed form 7, and is required to give the same information as in England and, in addition, the time of the stillbirth and, where applicable, the place of the parents' marriage.

Certificate of registration

There is no direct equivalent in Scotland of a disposal certificate.

After registration, the registrar issues to the informant a certificate of registration, which should be given to the undertaker to give to the keeper of the burial ground or to the crematorium authorities, as the case may be. There is no charge for this certificate.

Death certificates

As in England, the registrar issues, free of charge, a certificate of registration of death which can be used for national insurance purposes only. All other death certificates must be paid for.

The full copy of an entry in the register (the standard death certificate) costs 50p, including a 20p search fee, and 30p for each further copy ordered at the same time. A search will not be done for a period of more than ten years.

The other death certificates cost the same as in England. There are a number of different certificates for various special purposes similar to those in England, except for the certificate needed for encashing national savings certificates, savings in the post office national savings bank and premium bonds. In Scotland, a certificate is not issued for encashing these. Anyone requiring a death certificate for cashing national and post office savings should write to the director of savings, savings bank division, Blythe Road, London W44 1SB, requesting an application form for a death certificate in order to encash the deceased's savings, specifying that he requires the scottish form.

The application form should be completed and sent or taken with a 10p fee to the registrar where the death was registered. The reverse side of the form is printed to resemble an entry of death in the register and the registrar completes it by extracting the particulars from the register. He sends it to the director of the post office savings department, in the envelope which the applicant should give him.

In order to get a 10p death certificate for claiming from a trustee savings bank, you must provide the registrar with a statement, signed by an officer of the bank, that the certificate is required for savings bank purposes.

Death certificates are always obtainable from the registrar of the district where the death was registered; they are also obtainable from the registrar general, New Register House, Edinburgh EH1 3 YT, at any time after about a year to 18 months from the date of registration.

In this country the dead are either buried or cremated.

If the deceased has left no specific instructions, the decision what to do with the dead body is normally made by the executor or the next of kin. If there is neither, the person entrusted by the hospital or local authority to deal with the funeral arrangements has to decide about the disposal of the body. If you put any directions about the disposal of your body in your will, tell your executors or nearest kin too, in case the will is not read until after the funeral. Although it is usual to carry out any wishes the deceased had expressed about the disposal of his body, there is no legal obligation to do so.

Bequest of eyes

Corneal grafting is a technique of modern eye surgery which helps to cure blindness or defective sight. People wishing to bequeath their eyes for this purpose should write to the secretary of their nearest eye hospital, or to the Royal National Institute for the Blind (headquarters: 224 Great Portland Street, London W1N 6AA; in Scotland, the Scottish National Federation for the Welfare of the Blind, 39 St Andrew's Street, Dundee).

The four bequest forms you will be sent are simple to complete. One you keep, one you should give to your executor, one to the family doctor, and the other to the Royal National Institute for the Blind. Your next of kin should be told and asked to promise to carry out your wish. If you go into hospital as an inpatient, you should tell the ward sister of your bequest.

After your death, the doctor must be notified immediately so that he can make the necessary arrangements. It is essential that the eyes are removed within a matter of hours and the eye hospital doctor may come to take them even before the family doctor has arrived. If the death is being reported to the coroner, the eyes should not be removed without his approval.

If at the time when you die enough eyes are already available for the eye operations then being undertaken, or you die too far away from one of the centres where eye operations are being performed, your eyes will not be used.

Bequeathing a body

You can leave instructions that your body shall be given for medical research or teaching before finally being buried or cremated. Your executors or next of kin may nevertheless not do so because no one can own a body once it is dead and such a bequest is therefore not legally enforceable. (On the other hand, unless you have specifically said that you do not want this to happen, your executors or next of kin can give your body for medical purposes after your death.) You can, and should, make the arrangements yourself about bequeathing your body to a medical school, but also tell your executors and your nearest family, because they will have to act quickly after you have died.

You can write to the professor of anatomy at your nearest university medical school, or direct to HM Inspector of Anatomy at the Department of Health and Social Security, Alexander Fleming House, Elephant and Castle, London SE1 (in Scotland, at the Scottish Home and Health Department, 12–14 Carlton Terrace, Edinburgh EH7 5DG). No forms are sent to you to sign; forms will be sent to your next of kin or executor after your death.

Offers of bequests are not usually accepted from people under the age of fifty, because their life expectancy is at least 20 years more.

No guarantee is ever given that a body will be accepted. Medical schools in highly populated areas receive many bequests and if a number of donors die about the same time, some bodies may have to be refused. Another reason for refusal by a medical school may be the cost of transport; some medical schools do not accept bequests from farther away than 20 to 30 miles. However, medical schools in sparsely populated areas often find their work hampered by lack of bodies and the form of bequest to one medical school may allow the transfer of the body to another school which more urgently requires bodies for teaching and research.

Through the Department of Health you can donate your body generally, without specifying the medical school. The Inspector of Anatomy knows the requirements of all the medical schools in the country at any one time.

When the donor dies, the Inspector of Anatomy or medical school should be told immediately, if possible by telephone. A few questions will be asked about the circumstances of the death. The body may be refused for a number of reasons, such as if it has been the subject of a post mortem or if death followed a recent operation or is being investigated by a coroner.

If the body is accepted, the executor or next of kin should complete and return the form sent by the Department of Health. If the body was donated to a provincial medical school, the form must be sent to the anatomy department of the school. These forms ask the name and age of the deceased, date of death, and the address from which the body should be collected. If a special medical certificate was sent to the donor when he made the bequest, this must be completed and signed by the deceased's doctor. If the bequest is made through the Inspector of Anatomy, this special medical certificate should be sent to the Department of Health together with the other form.

Soon afterwards, either the medical school to which the body has been specifically bequeathed by the donor or, in London, the Department of Health, will send an undertaker to remove the body. Before that time the death must be registered in the usual way because the undertaker has to take away with him the registrar's disposal certificate. If the arrangement for leaving the body had been made direct with the medical school, the undertaker who comes for the body will take away with him the special medical certificate, and the medical school's forms confirming the bequest which the executor or a relative has to sign.

If the body is eventually to be cremated, the executor must also complete and sign the statutory application form for cremation, which he can ask the medical school to send.

The family and executor need make no further arrangements: it is the responsibility of the medical school to arrange burial or cremation when the time comes. A body used for teaching or research must be buried or cremated within two years. Some medical schools allow the next of kin, if they wish, to make arrangements themselves for a private funeral. Otherwise, the medical school arranges and pays for a simple funeral, and claims the state death grant. Unless instructions have been given by the person handing over the body that no ceremony be held, a service is conducted at the funeral by a minister or priest of the faith professed by the deceased. If burial or cremation in some place other than that normally used by the medical school or if particularly elaborate arrangements are requested, the extra expenses must be met by the relatives or executor. After a burial, some medical schools put up over the grave a simple headstone with the name and the year of birth and death of the deceased. The cost of any other type of headstone or memorial must be borne by the relatives. If a medical school does not put up a headstone, the grave can be located by its number in the cemetery records.

Some medical schools give no option on the method or procedure of disposal. In fact, some make it a condition that there shall be no contact later between the executor and the medical school.

Burial in churchyards

In theory, everyone, whether christian or not, has the right to
be buried in his parish churchyard. In practice, there may be
no space left in the churchyard, and appropriate fees have to
be paid. The land which is used as a graveyard around a Church
of England parish church is administered by the incumbent
(vicar or rector). Many old churchyards are closed for further
burials. Some churches have burial grounds separated from the
church where parishioners have the right of burial.

Parish boundaries are marked on local one-inch ordnance
survey maps. Everyone whose permanent address is within the
parish is entitled to be buried there, even if he dies somewhere
else. If a boundary is altered, the parishioners' right to burial is
in the new parish. But if the new parish has no burial ground he
retains his right to burial in the old parish. People who have
moved away to another parish may be denied the right to be
buried in the churchyard of their previous parish, even if the
new parish has no churchyard.

It is the incumbent (and his parochial church council) who
decides whether to allow someone who has no right of burial
in his churchyard to be buried there, and what fee to charge.
For a non-parishioner, or a stranger who dies when in the
parish, the burial fee is higher than for a parishioner.

The scale of maximum charges payable to the incumbent, to
church officials and to the parochial church council for funeral
services and burial in Church of England parishes is included in
the Parochial Fees Order 1962. This applies only in parishes
whose incumbent took office after the 1962 Order came into
force. The Order lays down fees for burial (excluding digging
charges) and for a funeral service in the church – the minimum
charge comes to £3·50.

The fee for the use of the organ is an extra, and the organist and
choir have to be paid in addition. You can be buried in a church-

yard without a religious service: this is unlikely to cost any less.

If the parish has its own gravedigger, he will dig the grave for a fee which the vicar lays down. Otherwise the undertaker has to find a gravedigger.

Paying a burial fee does not buy the right to choose the location of the grave in the churchyard. The vicar allots the site. Nor does the burial fee entitle you to ownership of the grave or to the exclusive right of burial in that grave.

If you want the exclusive use of a plot in a churchyard you must apply to the diocesan registrar to reserve a grave space, by a licence called a faculty. Although a faculty gives the right to say who can be buried in the plot, the freehold of the ground continues to belong to the church. The fee charged by the diocese for a faculty depends on the amount of work involved in the petition. It takes about six weeks for a faculty to be granted. When a person dies it is too late to get a faculty for him but his relatives could reserve the grave for other members of the family by a faculty. Anyone arranging a burial in a grave reserved by a faculty must produce the faculty or other evidence which proves his right to the grave. The incumbent charges a fee for the first and each subsequent interment in a grave reserved by faculty. Removing and replacing an existing headstone for subsequent interments in a grave will add to the cost.

On the plan of a parish churchyard all the graves should be numbered and the vicar should keep a record of who has been buried in each grave and which graves are reserved by faculty.

The parochial church council looks after the churchyard generally and keeps the paths and walks and unused parts tidy. When granting a faculty, some dioceses stipulate that a contribution, of about £10 or so, be made towards the upkeep of the churchyard. The family of anyone who is buried in a churchyard is responsible for looking after the grave.

Neither reserving a grave by faculty nor paying a burial fee gives you the right to put up a monument or other embellishment on the grave. For this, approval must be given by the incumbent and a further fee paid. The 1962 scale of charges includes the fees for permission to put up monuments. For a new stone monument, including an inscription, the fee amounts to at least £5.50. The charge for adding another inscription to an existing monument is £1. Permission to put up a small wooden cross costs 35p. The design and material of a monument must be approved in writing by the incumbent, and so must the wording of an inscription. Most parishes object to colloquialism and informal descriptions, such as 'grandad' and generally stipulate that any quotations should be from the bible.

The incumbent's authority to give permission for monuments and inscriptions is limited: anything other than a simple headstone or inscription requires a faculty.

When permission is given to erect a monument or memorial over a non-faculty grave, this does not confer exclusive use of the grave.

Burial in churches
Today, any rights an incumbent may have had in the past to consent to a burial inside his church building have become obsolete. Faculties to permit such burials are hardly ever granted and in urban areas burial in and under a church is prohibited by law.

If you want to put up a memorial inside a church you need to apply for a faculty for this.

Burial in cemeteries
If you want to be buried but not in a churchyard, you can be buried in a cemetery. Most cemeteries are non-denominational,

and run either by a local authority or by a company. A few cemeteries are owned by a particular denomination; these are generally restricted to members of that faith. All the local authority and some privately-owned cemeteries have a section of the ground consecrated by the Church of England, and a separate section of general ground. Some also have ground consecrated and reserved for other specific religious denominations. In most cemeteries, any type of religious service (or none at all) can be held. Most cemeteries have a chapel which is non-denominational, and provide a roster of clergy of different denominations.

Fees for burial in a cemetery vary widely even within the same locality. They are set by the owners, under the terms of the appropriate Acts of Parliament. Fees and regulations are usually displayed at the cemetery. If you write to the superintendents of the local cemeteries you will be sent lists or brochures (not always very easy to follow), from which you can compare the charges and conditions. One cemetery's fee may include the services of a clergyman; some do not allow flowers to be planted or put on graves; others do not permit any monument or memorial to be put up, except over the more expensive graves or for a limited number of years only after which the cemetery authorities can remove it. Conditions or payments for maintenance are often stipulated. Most local authority cemeteries have an application form which the executor or next of kin usually has to sign.

In most cemeteries there are various categories of grave. The cheapest are public (or common) graves. These are unmarked and the person paying the interment fee has no right to say who else may or may not be buried in the grave, and has no right to put up any kind of memorial.

However, some cemeteries allow you subsequently to buy the right of exclusive burial in such a grave, so that it becomes

a private (or purchased) grave. In some cemeteries no interments will take place in a common grave for a set number of
years – usually 7 or 14 – after the last burial, except to bury
there another member of the same family. In a few cemeteries,
for a small fee a grave space can be reserved for a set period –
say, 14 years from the date of payment. After this it reverts to
the cemetery unless a further fee has been paid either to reserve
the space for a further period, or for the exclusive right to the
grave on behalf of the person buried in it.

In most cemeteries you can pay for the right of exclusive
burial in a particular plot, in a similar way as by a faculty
granted for a grave in a churchyard. The right used to be in
perpetuity; nowadays it is more usually granted for a specific
number of years, for instance 50 or 75. For such a private grave
you get a deed of grant (sometimes referred to as a certificate
of ownership), for which some cemeteries make a separate
25p charge. Keep the deed somewhere safe and make sure your
executor or family knows where it is. It may have to be produced in evidence before the grave can be opened for an
interment. Usually the signature of the owner of the grave is
required on the cemetery's application form to authorise the
opening of a private grave. If the owner has died, the cemetery
will probably require some alternative formality to authorise
the use of the grave. Afterwards, the deed will be endorsed
with details of the burial and returned to the executors. An
interment fee has to be paid in addition, and also a fee for any
monument, kerbs, borders or other embellishment that may
be put up, as well as for removing and replacing an existing
headstone.

Another category of grave is the so-called lawn grave, in
which you have the right to exclusive burial but can put up
only a very simple headstone, leaving the rest of the grave
grass. These graves are always together in one part of the

cemetery. You pay less for this type of grave because it is easy to keep lawn graves tidy by mowing them all together. Again the interment fee is additional. You may not find lawn graves specified as such in a cemetery's list of charges and may have to ask whether there are any lawn graves.

The fees charged depend on the type, the size and the depth of the grave and, for a private or a lawn grave, also on its position (in other words how accessible it is).

On the plan of a cemetery the various categories of grave are shown (often by different colours), and you can find out from this plan which graves are available at the time.

A grave which is not lined but is cut into the earth without side support is called an earth grave. A brick grave has a bricked (or concrete) floor and walls and is more expensive than an earth one. To have a brick grave you must have the exclusive right in the grave. Some cemeteries charge a higher interment fee for a brick than for an earth grave and require longer notice for the burial. Formalities and the construction of a brick grave can take weeks. The standard size of a single grave varies slightly from cemetery to cemetery (for a private grave it is usually approximately 9 ft × 4 ft × 9 ft), and a grave larger than the standard size costs more. What is listed as a vault is in some cemeteries a bricked double grave, in others a grave bricked up to the level of the ground instead of to the top of the coffin.

In most local authority cemeteries a higher fee is charged (up to three times as much) for non-residents and non-rate-payers, though there may be some concessions for former residents and their relatives. Interment fees are less for children than for adults; each cemetery defines its own age limits.

All fees have to be paid in advance, and all the required documents sent to the cemetery a stipulated time before the funeral.

Each cemetery keeps a register of burials, and a record of

who owns a grave plot and who has already been buried in each grave. Copies of entries in the register can be bought at any time for a small fee.

Other burial grounds
If you want to be buried in ground other than a churchyard or cemetery, the law stipulates that such private burials must be registered. Even if you are the freeholder of the land, you must ascertain from the deeds whether the land is restricted in the use to which it may be put. If you want to bury someone in your garden, you must obtain permission from your local planning authority, and must give the local public health department an opportunity to object to your proposal. Finally, you must get approval from the Department of the Environment.

FOR BURIAL – THE DOCUMENTS

registrar's certificate for burial (the disposal certificate)	from registrar	free	required before burial can take place	via relative and under-taker to burial authorities. Part C returns to registrar
or after inquest: coroner's order for burial	from coroner	free	authorises burial	
for cemetery: application for burial	from cemetery via undertaker, usually signed by executor or next of kin	free	applies for burial and confirms arrangements	to cemetery authorities
grave deeds or faculty	from cemetery or diocese	varies	proves right to grave	to burial authorities
copy of entry in burial register	from burial authorities	10p to 15p	proves burial and locates grave	to executor or next of kin

Until 1965 it was illegal to cremate the body of anyone who had left instructions that he did not wish it. Now, however, there is no such restriction, and executors or next of kin are free to cremate or not as they choose. Even if the deceased had left specific instructions that he wanted his body to be cremated, there is no legal obligation on his survivors to carry out his wishes.

The Cremation Society (47 Nottingham Place, London W1) supplies forms on which to express 'an earnest desire to be cremated'. The Society will register this wish, free of charge, for anyone – not just members of the Cremation Society. The form is in two halves, one kept by the Society and one to be kept where the executors or next of kin would find it. A note to executors or family on a piece of plain paper is as valid but, because it looks less official, may be thought to be less effective.

By joining the Cremation Society (membership fee £7.35) or by taking out a policy with its related organisation, the Cremation Assurance Friendly Society, your dependants can claim £7.35 towards the cost of your cremation. The Society issues its members with a membership certificate and two identity cards (one to be kept by the member, and one to be put in an obvious place or given to someone likely to be responsible for the cremation). When arranging the funeral, whoever is in charge should give the certificate to the crematorium authorities who will then deduct £7.35 from the account.

If you take out a policy with the Cremation Assurance Friendly Society, you can pay an annual premium, the amount depending on your age when taking out the policy, until you are seventy or for a minimum of 10 years, whichever is the longer. When you die, your dependants claim a lump sum (a minimum £60). If you die before you have completed the requisite number of premium payments, a reduced sum is paid. This payment is irrespective of whether you are cremated when the time comes.

The Cremation Society is a registered charity. If you pay £7.35 outright as your membership fee, this is in practice an interest-free loan to the Society. The benefit your dependants will receive in the end is not more than the amount you paid in. Once you have undertaken to become a member of the Society you do not get the £7.35 back if you change your mind later on. Your family will not normally get a refund if your body is buried rather than cremated. But they will if it is accepted for medical research.

No one can be cremated unless the cause of death has been definitely ascertained. This means that, unlike burial which can be carried out on the authority of a disposal certificate issued before registration, cremation cannot normally be applied for until after the death has been registered or a coroner's certificate-for-cremation given.

Before cremation can take place, four statutory forms have to be completed, one by the next of kin, the others by three different doctors. The forms are issued by the crematorium; undertakers, as a rule, have a supply of them.

Form A is the application for cremation, and has to be completed by the next of kin or executor, and counter-signed by a householder who knows him personally.

Forms B and C and F are on the same piece of paper. B has to be completed by the doctor who attended the deceased during the last illness and who has to see the body before he can complete the form. The doctor will probably need to ask the relatives, or whoever was present at the death, for some of the information demanded on form B – for instance 'By whom was the deceased nursed during his or her last illness?', 'Did the deceased undergo any operation during the final illness or within a year before death?'.

Form C, the confirmatory medical certificate, has to be completed by a doctor registered in the UK at least 5 years, who must not be a relative of the deceased nor a relative or partner of the doctor who completed form B. The second doctor also has to see the body before he completes the form. Each of the doctors is entitled to a fee, often being paid there and then. The British Medical Association has recommended a minimum fee of £3.15, plus travelling expenses; in fact, fees of up to £5 and even more, are charged.

Forms B and C are not required when a coroner has issued a certificate-for-cremation. When a death is reported to the coroner you must let him know from the outset if you want the body to be cremated, so that his authority to dispose of it will be in the form of a certificate-for-cremation (otherwise you may have to go back to him to get the proper certificate). In the rare cases when the coroner has reason for not allowing the body to be cremated, he will not give a certificate-for-cremation but will issue an order for burial instead. The next of kin must accept this, or wait until he does authorise cremation.

Forms B and C are also not required for cremation of a body which has been used for medical research or teaching. In these circumstances the medical school's professor of anatomy completes the statutory form (form H or form 2) which takes the place of forms B and C.

The final authority to cremate the body is given on form F, signed by yet another doctor, the medical referee of the crematorium. He usually does so on the basis of the medical evidence of forms B and C, or H, or after he has received a coroner's certificate-for-cremation. The medical referee has the power to refuse authority to cremate, and if he cannot be fully satisfied through forms B and C, he may himself order a post mortem or refer the matter to the coroner. The relatives of the deceased have no right to prevent this. If they do not want a post mortem to be held, they will have to forgo cremation and have the body buried instead. If they agree to the post mortem, they will have to pay for it (unless, in rare cases, the crematorium does so).

If the body of a stillborn child is to be cremated, a special medical certificate has to be completed by a doctor who was present at the stillbirth or who examined the body. No second medical certificate is required. The crematorium's medical referee has to complete his form of authority to cremate.

The purpose of all these forms is to prevent any body being cremated while there are any possible doubts about the circumstances of the death.

Most crematoria produce at least one other form on which the person organising the funeral confirms any details already provisionally arranged, such as the date and time of cremation. Some crematoria ask for specific instructions about the disposal of the ashes on this form, others have yet another form for this.

The forms have to be submitted to the medical referee of the crematorium by a stipulated time – never less than twenty-four hours – before the cremation is due. The reservation of a time for the cremation is accepted subject to the forms reaching the crematorium within the specified time limit and the fees being paid in advance. Each crematorium has its own scale of fees and there is considerable variation between them. Some do not cremate at the weekend, others make an additional or double charge for cremation on a saturday or sunday or after normal hours. Some crematoria penalise latecomers by moving the cremation to the end of the day and charging an extra fee. Many crematoria have brochures giving details of what they offer and their charges. The fees for an adult range from approximately £5 to £12 and for a child (depending on age) from about £3 to £6. Some crematoria charge a reduced fee for people too old to be eligible for a state death grant.

The charge for a cremation usually includes the fee for the medical referee's signing of form F and the use of the crematorium's chapel, whether you hold a service there or not. The chapel is non-denominational. Most crematoria have a roster of chaplains of various denominations so that a suitable chaplain is available at any time. The chaplain's fee is likely to be about £1. In some crematoria it is included in the total fee, and if you take along your own clergyman, priest or minister, he claims his fee direct from the crematorium, not from you. Recorded music in the crematorium chapel is usually included, and so is an organ voluntary. At the time of arranging the cremation, you can ask for the organist to play a particular piece of music, but you cannot normally choose the recorded music. As crematoria work to a strict appointments system, any service has to be fairly short, unless a special booking is made for a longer period.

Some crematoria have a room which they call a chapel of rest where the body can be taken to await cremation. Any charge made for this is about 50p to 75p a day. Relatives or friends can go to see the body there during the crematorium's visiting hours.

If you do not wish it, there is no need to have a religious service at the crematorium, but you should make this clear at the time of booking. The coffin need not then pass through the crematorium chapel at all.

The process of cremation starts with the coffin going first into the committal room, to await cremation. The body is not taken out of the coffin, and each coffin is burnt individually in a cremator (which is what the special type of furnace is called). After about an hour to one and a half hours, the ashes are taken from the cremator and reduced further to a fine powder-like ash.

The majority of crematoria are run by local authorities.

Each crematorium has to keep a register of its cremations. You can get a certified copy of an entry in the register for a charge of about 25p; you are only likely to need such evidence if for some reason the death has not been registered in this country.

There is no law regulating the disposal of cremated remains. The crematorium will keep them free of charge for a limited time, usually a month. Then, in the absence of any special instructions, the ashes are either buried or scattered, whichever is the practice at the particular crematorium. The basic fee in many crematoria includes scattering or burial, otherwise this costs from about 25p to £2 extra. A crematorium charges more than its normal fee for scattering ashes from a cremation elsewhere. If you ask the crematorium to keep ashes for a period longer than the time ashes are kept free, there will be a charge of about 25p to 50p a month.

A crematorium scatters or buries ashes in what it calls its garden of remembrance. The ground there is usually not consecrated and the place is not marked. The deceased's family can ask to witness (in some crematoria for a fee) the proceedings, but there is no formal ceremony.

If a relative wants to take away the ashes, they can be collected from the crematorium about two hours after the cremation, in a container for which a charge of about 50p is made. For a similar fee (plus postage) the crematorium will post the ashes to the person who applied for the cremation. Because the ashes are in the form of very fine powder, they are usually sealed in a polythene bag inside the container, to prevent any escaping.

The person taking away the ashes may have to sign a receipt for them and state how they will be finally disposed of.

With the ashes the crematorium gives or sends a certificate which confirms that the cremation has taken place. This certificate is usually free and will be required by the church or cemetery authorities who are going to bury or scatter the ashes.

Ashes can be buried in most churchyards and cemeteries. Some have a separate section for this. The interment fee for burying ashes in a churchyard or cemetery is normally less than for a body. Burial of ashes is sometimes permitted in a churchyard which has had to be closed for ordinary burials, but a faculty may be required. Usually ashes are buried in a container; in some places they are funnelled direct into the ground. You may be allowed to set a small plaque into the ground or nearby wall to mark the place in the churchyard where the ashes were put. Some churches keep a book of remembrance inside the church, in which an entry costs about £2.

Alternatively ashes can be scattered, anywhere, provided it is not done too flamboyantly. The Church of England has certain stipulations about the disposal of ashes in consecrated ground: if not interred, the ashes must be strewn rather than scattered.

About a week after the cremation, the crematorium will probably send a brochure telling you what memorials are offered, with prices. These extras are optional – there is no need to have them.

In some crematoria there is a cloister or colonnade, called a columbarium, full of niches. A niche may be rented or bought and the ashes are either walled in by a plaque or left in an urn in the niche. There is no more space left in some columbaria; the charge at some crematoria still renting out niches is high.

Hand-lettered inscriptions in the book of remembrance, which is kept at the crematorium, usually cost a minimum of £2 for a two-line entry consisting of the name, date of death and a short epitaph. The crematorium displays the book open at the right page on the anniversary of the death (not of the date of cremation) for a limited number of years. Some crematoria offer a miniature reproduction of the entry in the book of remembrance, in the form of a card or bound as a booklet. The price of the booklet depends mainly on the luxury of the binding and is unlikely to be less than £2.

The charges for the erection of plaques or for inscriptions on panels in cloisters or memorial halls vary between crematoria. A number of local authority crematoria, however, allow no memorials other than an entry in the book of remembrance.

Some crematoria allow trees, or more usually rosebushes, to be planted over the spot where ashes are buried or scattered, or allow plaques or memorial seats to be put in the gardens. Again, costs vary, as does the length of time for which the crematorium will see to the maintenance.

Apart from the gardens of remembrance at crematoria, there are privately-run gardens exclusively for the burial of ashes. A plot can be bought in perpetuity; the cost varies from around £55 to over £500.

FOR CREMATION – THE DOCUMENTS

registrar's certificate for cremation (the disposal certificate)	from registrar	free	required before cremation can be applied for	via relative and under-taker to crematorium authorities. Part C returns to registrar
or after post mortem or inquest: coroner's certificate-for-cremation	from coroner	free	authorises disposal of body (supersedes forms B and C)	
form A	from crematorium via undertaker, to be completed by executor or next of kin	free	applies for cremation and confirms arrangements	to crema-torium authorities
form B	from crematorium via undertaker, to be completed by deceased's doctor	£3.15 plus	certifies cause of death	to medical referee at crematorium
form C	from crematorium via undertaker, to be completed by a second doctor	£3.15 plus	confirms cause of death in form B	to medical referee at crematorium
form F	from crematorium, to be com-pleted by medical referee	usually included in crema-torium's charges	authorises cremation	kept by crematorium authorities
form—	from crematorium via undertaker, to be completed by executor or next of kin	free	confirms arrangements; gives instructions for disposal of ashes	to crema-torium authorities
certificate for disposal of cremated remains (for burial)	from crematorium	usually free	confirms cremation and gives details of the death	via relatives to burial authorities
certificate of cremation	from crematorium	about 25p	copy of entry in register	to executor or next of kin

Undertakers

Whether the body is to be buried or cremated, many of the arrangements can be made by an individual on his own. But it is rare for a funeral to be carried out without the services of an undertaker.

The trade of undertaking has developed as a comprehensive business within the last 200 years when, in towns, some carpenters began to specialise in the production of coffins and some carriage proprietors started to concentrate on providing funeral carriages. Gradually, these functions merged and developed until the 'undertaking' of a funeral and its arrangements became a separate trade. Some firms of undertakers sub-contract by hiring hearse, cars, and bearers.

The status of undertakers was strengthened in the victorian era by the fashion for elaborate, often ostentatious, funerals. More recently, undertakers, who had come to be described as the dismal traders, banded together into a national association to counteract this image and to establish a code of ethical behaviour by means of which they could achieve some uniformity of conduct and practice among their members. The title of funeral director which they adopted was intended to complete the new image. The National Association of Funeral Directors sets examinations which its members can take, but membership of the Association does not depend on passing these examinations.

The undertaker's purpose is to assume total responsibility for organising and supplying the necessities for a funeral. The transaction is a business deal and even though it may be difficult for the next of kin or executor to be businesslike in the circumstances, it should be treated as such. Hard-hearted though it may seem, whoever is in charge of the funeral would be well advised to get in touch with more than one undertaker.

It is not part of an executor's formal duty to supervise or

authorise the funeral arrangements. The family should agree who is to be responsible, and since an executor is often a close member of the family, he or she may be the most suitable person to be in charge of the funeral arrangements.

Arrangements for the funeral should not be confirmed until the disposal certificate from the registrar or coroner is available, to be given to the undertaker.

At the time of asking an undertaker to quote you should have a fairly clear idea of what kind of funeral is wanted and how much can be spent on it. Some people insure during their lifetime for their funeral, or join one of the special friendly societies which pay out a lump sum on death. When an undertaker asks whether the deceased was insured in this way, and for how much, he then has a better idea of how much the funeral should come to. But usually the cost of a funeral is paid out of the deceased's estate – the money and property he left. If you intend to spend no more than a limited amount, tell the undertaker and ask what he is prepared to provide for that figure. Do not be persuaded into anything you do not really want, even if he assures you that everyone else has this or that. The undertaker is in business and is justified in trying to sell as many of his services as he can.

You can have preliminary discussions with the undertaker on the telephone, but to make the final arrangements he will have to come to you or you will have to go to his office. If the undertaker comes to the house, he will be in a position to suggest the standard and type of funeral which he considers to be in keeping with your standards and status.

In most cases the member of the undertaker's staff with whom you have the first interview remains in charge for the whole funeral. One of the first things he will want to know is where the body is and whether it is to remain there. If there has been a post mortem you must get the undertaker to fetch the body from the mortuary. If he has to send someone to lay out or take away a body in the middle of the night or at the weekend, he will charge extra.

If the body is to remain in the house rather than await the funeral at the undertaker's, he will arrange for it to be laid out if the nurse or any member of the family has not already done so. A nurse refers to laying out as the 'last offices', the undertaker calls it the 'first offices'. If the undertaker takes the body away without having laid it out, he will want to know what to do with clothing, and any jewellery, that he takes off the body and will ask what he should dress the body in – shroud or robe, or the deceased's own nightwear.

When he comes to collect a body from the house or a hospital, the undertaker uses either a covered stretcher, or a form of coffin which is called a shell. He takes the body away in a small hearse, in an ambulance, or in an anonymous-looking van known in the trade as a handy. In order to remove a body from a hospital, the undertaker usually has to have some written authority, such as the disposal certificate or an authorisation form signed by an executor or relative.

An increasing number of undertakers keep the body on their premises until the time of the funeral. Usually relatives (and, with their permission, friends) can go to see the body in what is variously called a chapel of rest, reposing room or slumber room. With some undertakers you have to make an appointment beforehand. Some undertakers also have their own chapel for private prayer in which a religious service can be held at the beginning of the funeral, before going to the cemetery or crematorium.

Embalming
Because it is easier to deal with a body when it has been embalmed, many undertakers like to embalm the body and

some insist on doing so. They are likely to call it preservative or hygienic treatment. If you do not want the body to be embalmed, tell the undertaker, because some embalm any body brought to their premises without specifically asking the family about it. Before a body is embalmed the doctor must have given his medical certificate of cause of death, and it would be unwise to embalm until a disposal certificate has been given. If the death is reported to the coroner, the body must not be embalmed until he has given his authority. If the body is to be cremated, the two doctors must have completed the forms for cremation before the body is embalmed.

Embalming, which is intended to delay the process of decomposition, involves replacing blood with a solution of formalin. It is temporary and is not to be compared with the ancient egyptian process of mummification. In this country embalmers tend not to use cosmetics, nor try to create a lifelike appearance. A body can be embalmed at home, but usually the embalming is done at the undertaker's.

In a mortuary, the bodies are kept refrigerated, and some undertakers use this method of preservation instead of embalming. When relatives come to see the body, it is brought from the cold room to the undertaker's chapel or to one of the reposing, slumber or rest rooms.

Funeral costs
Most undertakers nowadays offer what they call a complete or inclusive funeral. But as this includes only the bare minimum, it is as well to establish what services the undertaker is supplying for the stated price, and how much any additional items would cost. Different firms will include different items in their inclusive charge, but all include a coffin, a hearse and one following car up to a stated mileage, the bearers to carry the coffin and the services of an undertaker. There is no break-

down given of the cost of these services, which each undertaker assesses according to his own overheads and profit margin.

The price quoted for a complete funeral is based on the type of coffin. The undertaker should be able to show you illustrations of the different coffins and caskets he can supply. A casket is rectangular, instead of the traditional tapered shape of a coffin, and is always more expensive than a coffin. The wood, too, affects the price. Elm is usually the cheapest, japanese oak and mahogany the most expensive. Coffins and caskets are always lined. The linings and other fittings, such as pillows and handles, vary considerably according to the price the undertaker charges for his coffins. Handles can be expensive, especially if made of brass, and are in many cases ornamental and not used for carrying the coffin (except at jewish funerals). Many undertakers buy plain coffins from a wholesaler or coffin-maker and keep their own stock of handles, linings and other fittings, which they fix to each coffin when it is ordered. A nameplate is nearly always put on a coffin when the body is in it, giving the name, the date of death and the age of the deceased.

In victorian and edwardian days, it was the practice of the upper classes to use a kind of double coffin, the inner one being a lighter cloth-finished version of the solid, more elaborate outer one. The first cremation coffins were replicas of these inner ones. When an outer coffin was also used at a cremation, the inner case was taken out and the body cremated in it; the outer coffin was not burned (and was sometimes used again).

Nowadays for cremation it is usual to have a simple and unvarnished coffin, with handles and fittings not made of metal. It should therefore be at the cheap end of the price range. It is sometimes covered with a pall throughout the funeral.

If you choose one of the undertaker's more expensive coffins you will get a more elaborate standard of funeral. The prices quoted by undertakers for a so-called complete or inclusive funeral range from not much less than £50 to over £100.

A funeral often involves costs not covered by the under-taker's price for a complete funeral: laying out the body (up to £3.15), removing the body from the house or hospital to the undertaker's (about £3 to £5, but up to £12 if a removal has to be done outside normal working hours), embalming (£2 to £6), use of the undertaker's premises (about 75p per day), shroud or robe, and additional mileage if the hearse or cars have to go beyond the undertaker's mileage limit (up to 27p a mile). If he does an extra journey – to take the coffin to a church the night before the funeral, for example, or to fetch the body from the mortuary after a post mortem – there will be an extra charge. If extra following cars are required, these will cost another £3 to £5 each.

The National Association of Funeral Directors has a mini-mum funeral service scheme for a very simple funeral with a plain coffin. The Association has agreed that its members should not charge more than £64 (exclusive of the burial or cremation fees) for this basic minimum funeral. Some undertakers charge less. The belief that undertakers' charges vary according to the apparent wealth of their clients has not been disproved.

Most undertakers are prepared to give a quotation, and this should include itemised details of costs and should be in writing. Even if you 'leave it to him' you should get from him an estimate of the likely cost and what later additions (for instance, extra cars) will cost. Tell the undertaker not to incur such expenses without your authorisation – funeral guests may ask him to drive them to the railway station twelve miles away, or the clergyman require to be picked up by car.

Church, cemetery or cremation charges have to be paid on top of the undertaker's bill, and so do all other payments such as fees for clergyman and organist. The undertaker ought to be able to tell you the charges and conditions of the different churches, cemeteries and crematoria in his area. When comparing the scales of charges in the district, remember that undertakers' charges increase with the distance the funeral has to go.

Generally, the total cost of a funeral, including burial or cremation fees, is unlikely to come to less than £75.

The price levels vary between different parts of the country (for instance, prices tend to be higher in the south), as well as varying between local firms. A number of local consumer groups has carried out surveys of funeral costs in their areas, and published the results in their group magazines.

– stillbirth

A stillborn child does not usually have a funeral, but undertakers will arrange the disposal of a stillborn child. The charge for this is likely to be about £5 to £7 and includes cemetery or crematorium fees. The undertaker collects the body, takes it to his premises, provides a suitable coffin, and has it cremated, or interred in a public grave, without any ceremony.

Final arrangements

The undertaker must have the registrar's disposal certificate (or the coroner's equivalent authorisation) before confirming the final arrangements. He will see to it that all official forms are completed and taken to the right people at the right time. For a burial, for instance, he takes charge of any grave deeds and gets a cemetery's form of application signed by the executor. For a cremation, he sees that a relative or the executor completes the form of application and the form giving instructions for disposal of the ashes. He will also arrange for two doctors to complete forms B and C and pay out their fees and, when he has gathered the necessary forms, he will get them to the medical referee at the crematorium in time.

The fees to the vicar, sexton, gravedigger, organist, choirmaster, chaplain and officials at the cemetery or crematorium, as the case may be, usually have to be paid in advance. The undertaker will make the actual payments and will add the charges to his total account.

In effect, the undertaker should co-ordinate the various operations at the different stages. He will approach the people in charge of wherever it has been decided the burial or cremation is to take place (this usually means the local clergyman or superintendent of the cemetery or crematorium) in order to reserve a time and, for a burial, to order the type of grave you want. He can also be asked to make the arrangements for whatever service is to be held. Either the undertaker or a member of the family should first of all ask whoever the family wants to officiate at any service, whether he is willing to do so and whether he will be available at the time planned for the ceremony.

Most religious denominations have some form of funeral ceremony. In this country, unless the dead person had professed another religion, the Church of England service will probably be said at his funeral. Rituals can be adapted according to the preferences of those concerned. For instance, the main part of the service can be said in the church or at the undertaker's (with only a few words of committal at the graveside) or all the service can be at the grave. A funeral address may be given either in the church or outside, or not at all. A service in a crematorium or cemetery chapel is restricted by the time allowed – normally less than half an hour.

Anyone who specifically does not want any form of religious service must make this very clear to whoever is going to make the funeral arrangements. Although not customary, there is no reason why a body cannot be buried or cremated without any form of religious ceremony. If a body is to be buried in a churchyard without a religious ceremony (or with one, but held by a minister of another denomination), the incumbent of the parish is supposed to be given forty-eight hours' notice in writing. In practice, most vicars would give permission if asked over the telephone. The usual parish regulations apply and fees have to be paid.

If there is to be no service at a cemetery or crematorium, all that needs to be done is to arrange with the authorities the day and time of the funeral. The fee, particularly at a crematorium, may include a charge for the use of the chapel even though it is not used. Most cemeteries permit a non-religious ceremony to be held at the graveside, provided this is done in a reasonably dignified way. The British Humanist Association in London will provide someone to officiate and to give an address for a fee of £5 plus expenses. The National Secular Society also will, but their fee is not fixed.

Denominational burial grounds usually insist on their own form of service. If you are involved in arranging the funeral of someone of a faith different from your own, get in touch as soon as possible with the equivalent of the local parish priest of that denomination, to find out what needs to be done. With orthodox jews, for example, the body should be buried as soon as possible once the disposal certificate is issued. If a man subscribes to a synagogue burial society, he or his wife or his dependent children will be buried, free, by the society in its cemetery. The funeral and coffin will be very simple, and there will be no flowers. Orthodox jews do not get cremated, and embalming or bequeathing a body for medical purposes is not allowed. Non-orthodox jews are more flexible and there is less difference between their funerals and those of other denominations. The funeral will always be simple, but flowers are allowed and so is cremation. Not all non-orthodox synagogues have a subscription system for their burial society; with those who do not, the funeral cost is paid by the family. A synagogue sometimes agrees that its burial society may carry out the funeral of a jew who was not an active member of a synagogue and had not been subscribing to any burial society, but his family will be charged for the funeral and the cost will be considerably more than for an active member. There is rarely any difference between the funeral of members of the same synagogue; all are simple. If a jew dies away from home, it is the responsibility and expense of the relatives to bring the body back for the synagogue burial society to take over.

For a practising roman catholic, it is usual to arrange for the priest to say a requiem mass in the local parish church and for the body to lie overnight in the church beforehand. There are no set fees laid down for roman catholic priests to charge for their funeral services, but it is usual for the deceased's family to make an offering to the church. Cremation is now permitted for roman catholics, but some priests will not accompany the funeral to a crematorium, nor do all crematoria have roman catholic priests on their roster.

The funeral

You can arrange with the undertaker that the funeral shall start from your home or from his premises, usually depending on where the body is. Or you can ask him to take the body direct to the church, cemetery or crematorium for mourners to meet there. If the undertaker provides cars for the family and other special mourners, he will marshal the cortège and arrange when it shall start. Timing is important because the cemetery or crematorium authorities may add to, or even double, their charge if the funeral arrives late.

You should discuss and make a clear arrangement with the

undertaker beforehand about the procedure at the end of the funeral – for instance, whether you want him to take people home – and at what point you will not need him any more.

Before the undertaker puts the lid on to the coffin, he may ask the relatives or executors if they would like to witness this and see the body again (euphemistically, to pay their last respects). This also acts as a safeguard to check the identity of the body before finally closing the coffin.

At a burial preceded by a church service, the coffin is taken into the church by the bearers and placed in front of the altar. The mourners normally follow the coffin. In some anglican as well as most roman catholic churches, the coffin is taken into the church the previous evening, and remains there before the altar until the service. After the service, the bearers take the coffin from the church to the grave while the mourners follow, led there by a member of the graveyard or cemetery staff. If the service has been held elsewhere, or there is no service, the coffin is carried direct from the hearse to the grave.

At some more formal funerals there are pall bearers, who walk alongside the coffin but do not carry anything. Originally they used to carry the pall, a heavy canopy which was held over the coffin. Nowadays a form of pall is sometimes laid on top of a coffin to cover it during the service.

The bearers lower the coffin into the grave, on webbing slings, while the words of committal are said. The mourners sometimes throw earth on to the coffin, but they usually do not stay to see the complete filling-in of the grave, which is done later by the cemetery or graveyard staff.

Burying ashes in a churchyard or cemetery can be done with as much or as little ceremony as the relatives wish, by arrangement with the incumbent of the parish or with the superintendent of the cemetery.

Before a cremation, the service either takes place in a church with the words of committal said at the crematorium chapel, or the whole service is held at the crematorium. The coffin is taken into the crematorium chapel, followed by the mourners, and laid on the catafalque. As the committal sentences are being said, the coffin passes out of sight, either by being moved mechanically through a door, or by a curtain being drawn across it. You may be given an option for this not to happen until everyone has left the chapel, and in some crematoria there is no provision for removing the coffin during the service so that the mourners leave while the coffin is still in the chapel. If no religious service is being held, the coffin can be taken straight to the committal room between the chapel and the cremator.

The executors or next of kin can, when making arrangements for the cremation, ask to be allowed to go into the committal room to see the coffin placed in the cremator. Usually only two people are allowed.

If the ashes are not left to be scattered or buried at the crematorium, you can ask the undertaker to collect them and post or give them to you. Most undertakers offer a selection of urns or special boxes for you to put the ashes in. Or an undertaker will, for a fee, scatter the ashes for you in a suitable part of a park or garden. Some undertakers will, also for a fee, keep ashes until the time when they can be mingled with the ashes of, say, the husband or wife, to be scattered or buried together.

Arrangements such as these do not need to be made at the funeral. You can see the undertaker later.

After the funeral, light refreshments are sometimes provided for the mourners, usually in the house of a member of the immediate family, or the undertaker may make arrangements at a local restaurant. In the days when attending a funeral involved a long journey, and considerable time, a substantial meal had to be provided afterwards. Nowadays the funeral meal on a large scale is a rarity except in the north country.

The undertaker will send in his account fairly soon after the funeral. It may not be possible to pay until probate has been granted; he does not usually press for immediate payment. Most undertakers will accept payment by instalments without charging interest.

Some of the costs of a funeral arranged by a co-operative society on behalf of one of its members are eligible for any dividend payable.

The undertaker's account should be as detailed as possible, and show separately what is due to him for his services (and the coffin) and what he has paid out on your behalf. He should send you receipted bills for the burial or cremation charges, doctors' fees, and any other payments he made (such as the cost of any flowers you asked him to order). This will enable you to check that no tips or other extras were paid out except those you had specifically requested him to give. Tips to bearers, gravediggers, cemetery or crematorium staff could mount up considerably.

However, many of the payments that the undertaker will have made for you are expenses you would have incurred anyway. He may have inserted a notice in the newspaper on your behalf, or arranged catering for those who came to the funeral, or ordered special stationery to be printed.

Notices

Announcements of deaths are usually made in the national and local newspapers most likely to be read by the deceased's friends and acquaintances. Many newspapers, including the national dailies, will accept the text by telephone, provided the office can telephone back to read over to a member of the family or the undertaker the text that is going to be printed. The papers do not usually ask for evidence that the death has occurred, unless the notice is submitted by someone who is not a relative, or the executor, or the undertaker. When the undertaker inserts the notice on behalf of his client, he may take the opportunity to include his firm's name and address, usually as being able to supply more information about the funeral or to receive flowers beforehand. The cost of an announcement will be based on the number of lines the notice comes to. The national daily newspapers insist on a standard form of announcement: the family name of the dead person, the date of death and the place (the cause of death is not usually included, nor are the names of hospitals and nursing homes, except with their permission), the deceased's full name (but the papers exercise their editorial control strictly, even to the extent of excising nicknames), home address and often some mention of the remaining family.

Details of time, date and place of the funeral can be included. Anyone who has not been specifically invited but wishing to attend is expected to arrive independently at the time and place announced in the press. If the family wants to restrict attendance at the funeral, the notice should say 'funeral private' or 'no ladies'. When a funeral is announced as private, only those whom the family has asked to come should attend. If the relatives think that a great many people might wish to come, they may arrange for the funeral to be private followed by a memorial service some days or weeks later for all those who wish to pay tribute to the dead person. If no details of the time and place of the funeral are published at all, it is to be assumed that the funeral is to be a private one.

Flowers
The notice in the newspaper should also make it clear if no letters are wanted, or no flowers (sometimes only the family's, or only certain types of flowers are requested).

A 'no flowers' request should be strictly observed. Some-times other ways are suggested in which sympathy can be expressed; for example, by giving plants or shrubs to the cemetery or crematorium garden, or, more usually, by dona-tions in the name of the deceased to a particular charity or organisation in which he or she was interested.

On the other hand, the newspaper notice may specifically state where flowers should be sent. If they go to the undertaker (or direct to the cemetery or crematorium), it is important that the deceased's name should be clearly stated on the label. The undertaker will make a list of the people who have sent flowers, so that the next of kin have a record afterwards. He will tran-sport the flowers with the coffin to the church, cemetery or crematorium. When the body is buried, the flowers are left on the grave. A crematorium may restrict where flowers can be put (for instance, not on the coffin) and reserve the right to dispose of flowers afterwards.

By their very construction, funeral wreaths and ornamental flower displays are unsuitable for other purposes. Relatives sometimes specify 'cut flowers' or 'sprays' with the intention that these should be used afterwards for hospitals or similar establishments, and may ask (and pay) the undertaker to take them there after the funeral. But the fact that the flowers have been used at a funeral may make them unwelcome and, having been handled several times, they will probably be past their best.

Memorials

A headstone or other memorial in a churchyard or cemetery is subject to the restrictions imposed by the church or by the cemetery. The family or the monumental mason must apply to the church or cemetery authorities for permission to do anything to mark the grave, such as enclosing it by a kerb or railings, covering it with a slab or stones, placing flower vases or urns on it, putting up a headstone or erecting any other memorial. A copy of the entry in the burial register may be demanded or, if the grave is a private or faculty one, whoever is applying has to produce the deeds as authorisation and as a means of identifying the grave. The undertaker is not usually involved in these arrangements but he should warn you of any restrictions he knows about memorials when you are choosing between burial grounds. Some undertakers run a firm of monumental masons in addition to their undertaking business.

Do not commission a monumental stone mason to carry out any work for you without knowing what the burial ground's regulations are. There will be restrictions affecting the size, shape and material of any memorial and the words and lettering of an inscription. You should first obtain written permission for what is proposed. In a churchyard this may necessitate a faculty. You will have to pay a fee to the church or cemetery authorities, quite apart from the cost of the memorial itself. A simple headstone for a lawn grave is likely to cost at least £20 if made of plain english stone; marble memorials start at about £40, and coloured granite can cost £100 or more.

Normally a headstone cannot be erected, or replaced after a second burial, until the ground has settled over the grave, usually several months after the burial. Less reputable monumental masons, on finding out when a funeral is being held, importune the family with discreditable haste, even at the graveside or by calling at the house on the day of the funeral. They often ask for a deposit on the spot, and for a signature to confirm the order. Do not yield to their persistence and persuasiveness.

CHARTS

of what to do when someone dies

CHART 1

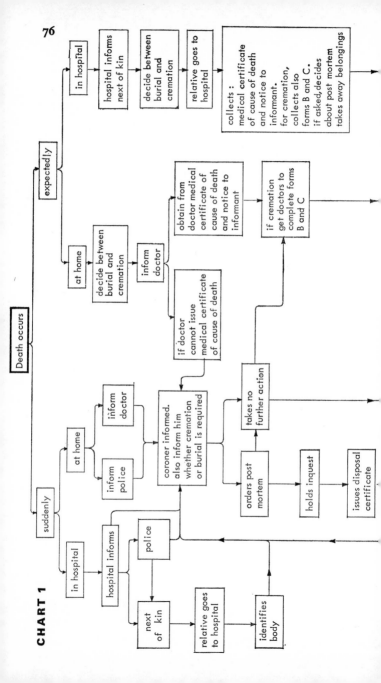

Death occurs

expectedly

in hospital → hospital informs next of kin → decide between burial and cremation → relative goes to hospital → collects: medical certificate of cause of death and notice to informant. for cremation, collects also forms B and C. if asked, decides about post mortem takes away belongings →

at home → decide between burial and cremation → inform doctor → obtain from doctor medical certificate of cause of death and notice to informant → if cremation get doctors to complete forms B and C →

if doctor cannot issue medical certificate of cause of death →

suddenly

at home → inform doctor / inform police → coroner informed. also inform him whether cremation or burial is required → takes no further action →

orders post mortem → holds inquest → issues disposal certificate

in hospital → hospital informs → police / next of kin → relative goes to hospital → identifies body →

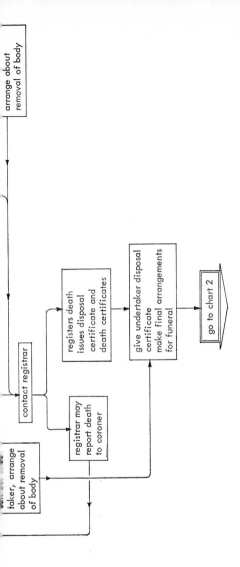

CHART 2

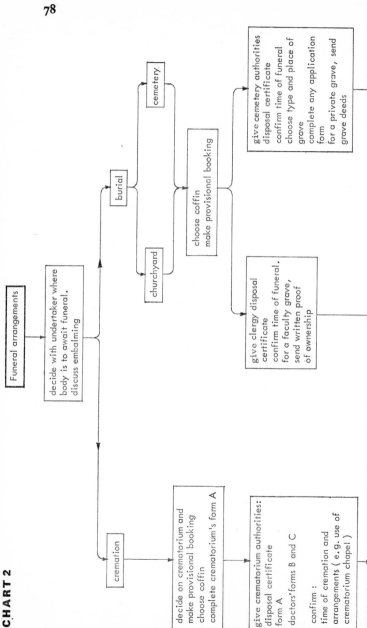

Funeral arrangements

decide with undertaker where body is to await funeral. discuss embalming

cremation

decide on crematorium and make provisional booking
choose coffin
complete crematorium's form A

give crematorium authorities:
disposal certificate
form A
doctors'forms B and C

confirm :
time of cremation and arrangements (e.g. use of crematorium chapel)

burial

churchyard

cemetery

choose coffin
make provisional booking

give clergy disposal certificate
confirm time of funeral.
for a faculty grave,
send written proof of ownership

give cemetery authorities disposal certificate
confirm time of funeral
choose type and place of grave
complete any application form
for a private grave, send grave deeds

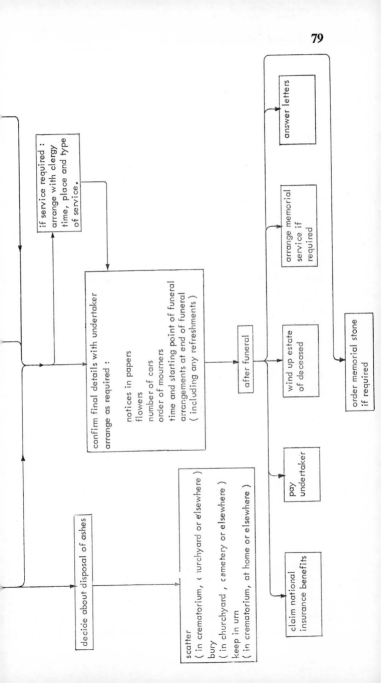

if service required :
arrange with clergy
time, place and type
of service.

confirm final details with undertaker
arrange as required :

notices in papers
flowers
number of cars
order of mourners
time and starting point of funeral
arrangements at end of funeral
(including any refreshments)

after funeral

wind up estate
of deceased

pay
undertaker

claim national
insurance benefits

decide about disposal of ashes

scatter
(in crematorium, (iurchyard or elsewhere)
bury
(in churchyard , cemetery or elsewhere)
keep in urn
(in crematorium, at home or elsewhere)

answer letters

arrange memorial
service if
required

order memorial stone
if required

Pre-death arrangements

If you want to make the arrangements personally for your own funeral you can approach an undertaker at any time and discuss with him what you want to happen when you die. He will refer to this as an NYD ('not yet dead') funeral and will file all the details you have agreed until the time comes to implement your directions. He may suggest that you sign a list of agreed arrangements and give a copy to your next of kin or executor. You can pay in advance towards the expenses but if costs rise in the meantime the undertaker will claim from your estate any additional amount which is due to increased costs. If you pay in advance it is the undertaker who gets the benefit of the interest on your money.

Funerals away

Some people express a wish to be buried near their family although they now live somewhere else. For this reason, or if someone dies in an area other than where he lived, funeral arrangements have to be made in two places. One under-taker will probably cope. If it is too far for him to supervise both ends himself, he may sub-contract arrangements at the other end to a colleague, but his contract with the other under-taker is not your concern. Alternatively, you can contact an undertaker in the district to which the body is to be taken and deal with him direct.

A body is sent by road in a hearse whenever possible because this is likely to be a quicker and cheaper means of transport. For long distances, it may be better to send it by rail, sea or air, but you then have to pay for a hearse at both ends of the journey. The basic rail charge is £7.50 for any journey up to 30 miles, then 25p a mile; the exclusive use of a guard's van or a locked compartment is extra. With the body must be sent the disposal certificate and other documents such as grave deeds. It is usual to embalm the body before sending it on its journey.

Sending a body abroad

Cremated remains can be sent anywhere without restrictions, and no official notice has to be given or permission sought when ashes are being taken out of the country. Restrictions may, however, be imposed by the authorities at the other end.

But if the body of someone who has died in England or Wales is going to be buried or cremated in another country (including Scotland, Northern Ireland and the Channel Islands), the coroner of the district in which the body is lying must be told. Form 104 gives 'notice to a coroner of intention to remove a body out of England'. You can get this from the registrar when registering the death, and ask him for the name and address of the coroner to whom it should be sent. If he knows in time that the body is going out of the country, the registrar will not issue a disposal certificate. If, however, a disposal certificate has already been given, it must be sent to the coroner when sending him form 104.

The coroner gives a formal acknowledgment of this notice. The body must not then be taken out of the coroner's area for 4 days. Provided the coroner does not in the meantime requisition the body for a post mortem or inquest, you can go ahead with your plans for removing the body once the four days from the date of the coroner's acknowledgment are up. The coroner can waive the four-day waiting period by specifically stating this in his acknowledgment. He may do so, for instance, at the request of the executor or next of kin, if for any good reason there is urgent need to move the body out of the country by a particular date.

An undertaker will make arrangements about moving the body with British Rail, any freight-carrying airline or any shipping line. Transporting a body can be expensive. Some airlines charge twice the normal cargo rate for a body in a coffin. There may be special requirements: for example, that the coffin is enclosed in a crate or that it is airtight. Most airlines insist on the body being embalmed. This requires a special kind of embalming, and a certificate of embalming must accompany the body. Also the necessary freight documents must be completed. The consular office of the country to which the body is going will know what regulations have to be met. You will need one standard form of death certificate for the UK customs, and another one, or more, depending on the requirements of the country to which the body is going. You may have to have all documents translated and authenticated at the consulate of the country concerned, for which you will have to pay. The consulate will also tell you what arrangements you can make beforehand and what formalities will be required on arrival of the body.

Burying a body in the sea is removal out of England or Wales, and the coroner must be informed accordingly. Anyone can be buried at sea at least 3 miles beyond the low water mark. The only document needed is the coroner's acknowledgment of the notice of intended removal.

The harbour master of the port you want to use should be able to suggest a suitable ship whose master knows the local tides and coast and who can therefore choose a position least likely to yield up the body once it has been committed. The cost is a matter of bargaining between you and the master of the vessel from which the body is to be launched. If a coffin is used, it needs to be weighted and have holes bored in it to make sure it sinks.

Bringing a body from abroad
When a british subject dies abroad, whether as a resident there

or as a visitor, his death must be registered according to local requirements and regulations. The british consul in that country can also register the death. The advantage of the death being registered by a british consul is that certified copies of the entry of death can eventually be obtained from the General Register Office in London, just as if the death had been registered here in the normal way. Otherwise no record of the death will be kept in this country.

If you want to get back to this country the body of a person who died abroad, you should ask the advice of the british consul there, or of the Foreign Office consular department in London. Some of the larger firms of undertakers have agents abroad and can arrange either to have a funeral in the other country, or to bring the body back here. Bringing a body back is likely to cost several hundred pounds. If the body is brought back, the UK customs require some evidence of the death to come with the body, such as a death certificate issued in the place where death occurred, or some official authorisation to remove the body issued by a local coroner (or equivalent).

Anyone arranging the funeral in England or Wales of someone who has died elsewhere, including Scotland and Northern Ireland, must supply the registrar of the district in which the body is to be buried or cremated with evidence that the death took place outside England or Wales. This evidence is either the british consul's authentication of a foreign death certificate or, if the death took place in Scotland or Northern Ireland, a death certificate issued there. The registrar of the district in England or Wales can then issue a certificate called the 'certificate of no liability to register'. This takes the place of the disposal certificate.

The body must be buried within a fortnight because part of this certificate of no liability to register must be returned within fourteen days to the registrar who issued it. If a body brought from outside the UK is to be cremated, a doctor's statement of the medical cause of death must be sent with it (this may have to be translated and authenticated). You or the undertaker should send or take the completed cremation application form A and all the documents which came with the body to the Home Office, Romney House, Marsham Street, London SW1. It is wise to telephone beforehand to check that you have all the necessary documents: the telephone number is 01-799 3488, extension 179. If you post them, put 'cremation urgent' on the envelope. The Home Office then issues a certificate to take the place of forms B and C for the crematorium's medical referee.

REMOVAL TO OR FROM OTHER COUNTRIES – THE DOCUMENTS

form 104 (notice to a coroner of intention to move a body out of England)	from registrar, to be completed by executor or next of kin	free	gives notice that body will be taken out of country	to coroner of place where body is
coroner's acknowledgment of removal notice	from coroner	free	confirms that body may be removed after four days	to executor or next of kin, to send with body
if death abroad: certificate of no liability to register	from registrar	free		
part A	to be completed by relative		declares details of death and applies for part B	to registrar
part B	to be completed by registrar		states that death is not required to be registered; takes place of disposal certificate	to relative who completed part A
part C	to be completed by burial or cremation authorities		confirms that burial or cremation has taken place	to registrar (within 14 days) who issued part B

When someone dies on a foreign ship or aircraft, it counts as a death abroad. On a british-registered ship or aircraft, the death is recorded in the captain's log for the day. Eventually a copy of the log entry can be obtained from the General Register Office in London.

If a member of the forces dies serving abroad, the Ministry of Defence arranges and pays for his funeral there. If the family prefers, it may be possible to fly the body home; once it has reached the undertaker in this country the family becomes responsible and has to pay for the funeral. The Ministry of Defence contributes a grant of £10, or £5 and a coffin. In some countries, the Ministry can arrange cremation if requested, and for the ashes to be sent home.

If a serviceman dies in this country, his funeral will also be arranged and paid for by the Ministry of Defence; burial will be in a military cemetery, or cremation can be arranged if requested. If the relatives prefer to arrange the funeral themselves, they will get the Ministry grant towards this.

Local authority funerals
When someone dies who has either no relatives or none able or willing to pay for the funeral, the hospital or the local authority of the area where the person died or where the body was found has to arrange the funeral, and if necessary to pay the costs. If the police have a body in their charge for which they cannot trace any relative, they notify the local authority who then has to arrange the funeral.

No arrangements should be made by anyone with an undertaker before getting in touch with the local authority health department or social services department. Most local authorities, hospital and similar management committees who may find themselves with the responsibility for disposing of a body have a contract with a local undertaker for a very simple funeral. The authority claims the cost of the funeral from any state death grant that may be due. The contract arrangement between the local authority and the undertaker usually keeps the cost so low that the death grant may actually be more than enough for the funeral. If there is any balance, the Department of Health and Social Security gives it to any next of kin.

Cases of hardship

The Supplementary Benefits Commission has no power to provide for funerals as such, but is nevertheless sometimes able to use its general powers of discretion in order to assist with the cost of a funeral in cases where someone who has already arranged a funeral would experience hardship if left to meet the expenses unaided. Normally, the Commission only helps people whose resources are such that they already receive supplementary benefit, and has to be satisfied that the expenses could not be met in any other way. Application should be made through the Department of Health and Social Security.

If someone who was receiving a war disablement pension dies as a direct result of that disablement, the Department of Health and Social Security may arrange and pay for a very simple funeral. The next of kin should contact the local war pensions office straightaway if they want the Department to take over. Alternatively, the Department will make a grant equivalent to the full state death grant for any such pensioner if he does not qualify for the full state death grant.

Presuming death

If the relatives of someone who has disappeared want to apply for a court order to presume that he has died, they must produce evidence that he is likely to be dead – for example, that he was known to have been in an area where there was an earthquake – or that they have gone to great lengths to try to find him. Usually relatives have to wait seven years before they apply, but not if the missing person was in an aeroplane that crashed or a ship that went down. The petition is made to the high court of justice, and, if granted, an order giving leave to presume death is made by the court and a copy can be used in place of death certificates or as evidence before another marriage.

Disposal

The certificate of registration of death which the registrar has given to the informant must be given to the person in charge of the place of interment or cremation. No part of the certificate is returned to the registrar.

Burial

In Scotland, as in England, it is possible to purchase the exclusive right of burial in a cemetery or kirkyard plot, either in perpetuity or for a limited period. Cemetery chapels are rare. Most kirkyards nowadays are administered by the social work department of the local authority. In Scotland, a grave is referred to as a lair.

At a burial, silk tasselled cords, called courtesy cords, are attached to the coffin. Specific mourners are sent a card beforehand inviting them to hold a cord while the coffin bearers take the strain of the lowering. Courtesy cords are not used for the burial of cremated remains.

A pad or mattress is often put on top of the coffin as a development of the old custom of putting grass or straw over the coffin to muffle the sound of the earth falling on the lid when the grave is filled in.

Cremation

The regulations and procedure for cremation are the same as in England and Wales since the Cremation Regulations 1965 brought these into line with those of Scotland.

Sending a body abroad

As in England, cremated remains can be taken anywhere without any restrictions and no formal notice has to be given or permission sought when ashes are being taken out of the country. There are no formalities connected with the removal of bodies out of Scotland either *or cremation or burial in another country. The procurator fiscal does not have to be informed.*

If the body is being taken to England or Wales for burial, the certificate of registration must be produced for the registrar there.

Bringing a body from abroad

There is no need to produce evidence for the registrar in Scotland that the death took place elsewhere. If the body is coming from England, he will require the coroner's acknowledgment of the notice of removal.

When a body is brought into Scotland to be cremated there, the authority of the Secretary of State for Scotland must be obtained before cremation can be carried out. This means applying to the Scottish Home and Health Department, 12–14 Carlton Terrace, Edinburgh EH7 5DG, with any supporting papers such as a foreign death certificate. Ashes brought into Scotland must be accompanied by a certificate of cremation issued by the crematorium.

None of the deceased's property should be sold nor, strictly speaking, given away until probate has been granted, or letters of administration. In the course of getting probate (if the person who died left a will) or letters of administration (if he died intestate), the deceased's personal representative must inform the bank, who will stop payment of all cheques and banker's orders; notify the post office, who will temporarily freeze any savings held there; and notify the tax inspector. After the grant of probate or of letters of administration, the personal representative will settle the debts, obtain payment of any life insurance policy, and transfer the ownership of any house, shares or other property the deceased may have had. (A detailed account of how to administer an estate is given in the Consumer Publication *Wills and probate*.)

The death grant should be claimed, and any other national insurance benefits that may be due.

The deceased's medical card should have been taken or sent to the registrar of births and deaths at the time of registering the death. So should any war service pension book.

All other pension and allowance books of the deceased must be returned either to the issuing office quoted in the book or to the Department of Health and Social Security. If there are any uncashed orders which are due, they must not be cashed after the death, even if they have already been signed. Any unpaid amounts should be claimed when the book is returned. To get any unpaid portions of a war pension, write to the Department of Health and Social Security, War Pensions Issue Office, Norcross, Blackpool, and claim the amount due, quoting the pension number. Unless the executors or next of kin make a specific claim, no repayments are offered by the Department for any outstanding pensions or allowances.

If the deceased had been an officer in one of the armed forces and a pension or allowance was being paid on the basis of his war service, the next payment that comes will have to be returned, uncashed, to the issuing office. Send with it a note of the date and place of death, and claim any amount that has become due since then.

If income tax was being deducted from the dead person's salary under the pay-as-you-earn scheme, a refund of tax may be due, depending on the date of death and whether tax had been paid up to then. Apply to the inspector of taxes for the area where the deceased's tax affairs were dealt with; if no one contacts him about a refund, he will not do anything about it (though the executor will hear from the collector of taxes if there is any tax due).

Responsibility may need to be transferred into the name of another person for a house or a flat. Relatives who were living with the deceased in rented accommodation should seek advice about their rights, from their citizens' advice bureau or a solicitor. (The landlord is not likely to be the best person to advise, because he may be motivated by his own interests.) If a widow or a relative who was living with the deceased should go away for any length of time, arrangements must be made for any rent or mortgage payments to continue. A widow, or anyone else, is eligible to apply for a rates rebate (even if the rates are not paid separately but are included in the total rent) if her income falls below a minimum average – from April 1972, £12 a week. The local council office can supply the application form for claiming a rates rebate.

If relatives have to arrange to clear a flat or house quickly, furniture which is not required can be offered to a local dealer or auctioneer, and anything which is not saleable will sometimes be accepted by local charities. If you have to arrange with the local authority refuse department to make a special collection, a charge may be made.

Sometimes following the announcement of a death in the papers, secondhand clothes dealers call round at the house and offer to buy the dead person's clothes. This is a simple way of getting rid of the clothes if you want to, although you will probably not be offered much for them. Remember to look through pockets and handbags before letting the clothes go. If you want to give the clothes to a charity, you will almost certainly have to pay the cost of getting them there. Some auctioneers have occasional sales of clothing. You have to get the clothes to the auction rooms and the auctioneer will send you the money paid for the clothes, minus his commission, a little while after the auction. Alternatively, you can advertise the clothes for sale, singly or as a complete wardrobe. In a similar way, other unwanted possessions of a dead person, such as books, cameras, sports equipment, can be sold by being advertised or offered to a local dealer or secondhand shop, or given to a charity.

When going through the dead person's belongings, you will probably find various tickets and documents. A rail season ticket should be taken to the station where it was issued and a refund claimed. If the ticket has not been used recently, either because the deceased had been ill for a long time before his death or because the ticket was not discovered until some time afterwards, the station will require evidence, such as a death certificate or doctor's certificate, before backdating the refund. To return a season ticket for the London underground and claim a refund, write to the fares and charges officer of the London Transport Executive. A widow or widower will probably be paid any refund direct, otherwise it is paid through a solicitor into the deceased's estate. London Transport require evidence before backdating a refund.

Send a passport back to the Passport Office, Petty France, London SW1, with a letter of explanation. A driving licence should be returned to the taxation office of the local authority; the logbook of a car must be returned too, for the change of ownership to be recorded. Insurance companies should be notified and asked to cancel any policies in the deceased's name and to refund any unexpired premiums.

There may be a refund to claim on unexpired memberships, so clubs and associations to which the dead person belonged should be told of his death and any unwanted subscriptions cancelled. Library tickets and any library books or records should be taken back to avoid getting a series of reminder cards and possibly a fine.

If the telephone was in the dead person's name, the executor or next of kin should write to the area telephone manager to tell him of the death and ask either for the telephone to be transferred to another name, or for the telephone to be disconnected and the account made up so that it can be paid out of the estate. To stop the deceased's mail coming to the house, the local postmaster should be asked to forward any mail to the executor. The telephone manager and the postmaster may ask for evidence of death, such as a death certificate.

Where necessary, the executor should also write to the local electricity and gas boards to cancel the deceased's contract with the board and to ask for the meter to be read so that the debt can be met from the estate. The boards should be told who will be responsible for the account, so that a new contract can be made.

A number of employers run pension schemes, sometimes linked to life insurance policies. When an employee dies, some schemes provide either a cash sum or a pension, sometimes both. Find out from the dead person's last employers whether any such payments are now due.

A widow or anyone else whose income is reduced below the guaranteed minimum weekly average can claim a supplementary allowance or pension. Explanatory leaflets (SP1 for people over retirement age, S1 for younger people) are kept at all post offices and include an application form. An officer of the Department of Health and Social Security will call, if asked, to discuss the position if the applicant does not want to go to the office to give the required information about his or her financial circumstances.

There are various societies, professional bodies, trade unions and ex-service organisations which run benevolent schemes for the dependants of their members or of people who qualify within the scope of the organisation. A widow should get in touch with the secretary of any organisation related to her husband's activities to find out what benevolent schemes might be available.

To help widows in practical and advisory ways, a series of voluntary groups called Cruse clubs have been set up in various parts of the country. Details can be obtained from Cruse, 6 Lion Gate Gardens, Richmond, Surrey; membership fee £1.

There are other local and national organisations whose activities include helping those who are alone. Some ask payment for their services, depending on the income of the person getting help. Some of these organisations are voluntary, others come under the local authority. Information about them may be obtainable from a local council of social service.

National insurance benefits are paid to the dependants of those who paid weekly national insurance contributions, or who had them credited while claiming sickness invalidity, injury, or unemployment benefit.

The Department of Health and Social Security administers all national insurance benefits. It issues explanatory leaflets for different categories of people and situations – for example, on widow's benefit and on the death grant – and these are available free at any Social Security office.

A record of every insured person's contributions is kept by the Department of Health and Social Security. You are not expected to know what contributions have been paid or credited when you apply for any benefits.

The number of contributions required varies according to the type of benefit claimed. When the number of contributions made does not qualify for a full benefit, there are sliding scales of reduced benefits. You can appeal through the local office if you do not agree with the decision about your claim.

Death grant
The death grant is a lump sum of £30 maximum. It is usually paid to the executors or to the next of kin, or to whoever is paying for the funeral.

Following the death of a man, a claim for the death grant can be based on either his own insurance record or that of his wife, whether she is still alive or not. If the contributions of one are not sufficient, the other's may be. Similarly, for a woman the claim can be based on her own insurance record or that of her husband, whether he is still alive or not. If a divorced woman had not remarried, her former husband's contribution record may be used to help meet the conditions.

For someone who because of mental or physical incapacity has never been able to work and pay national insurance con-

DEATH GRANT—*Conditions*

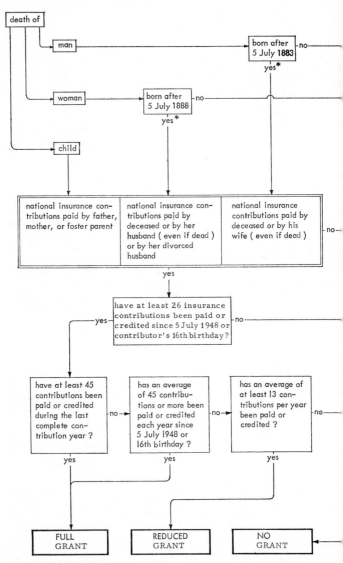

*reduced grant if born
within following ten years

tributions, a death grant may be paid on the insurance record of a close relative.

When a child dies, a claim can be based on the insurance record of either mother or father, even if dead, or of a foster parent. If the parents are separated or divorced, the claim is based on the insurance record of either parent. Anyone under school-leaving age, under 19 if a full-time student or an apprentice or unable to work because of illness, counts as a child in this context.

To qualify for the death grant, 45 contributions must have been paid or credited in the last completed contribution year. If fewer than 45 contributions were made in the last year, an average of 45 weekly contributions must have been made per year since 5 July 1948 (when the national insurance scheme started), or since the person concerned became 16, whichever is later. If the average comes to less than 45 per year but more than 13, a reduced death grant may be paid. No grant is paid if less than an average of 13 contributions per year has been paid or credited since 5 July 1948, or less than 26 in all.

The amount of the grant is also determined by the age of the person who died. No death grant is paid after a stillbirth. For a child up to three the grant is £9, for a child between three and five years it is £15, and for anyone between the ages of six and seventeen it is £22.50. From the age of eighteen, the death grant is £30 for a man who was born on or after 5 July 1893 and for a woman who was born on or after 5 July 1898. A man born between 5 July 1883 and 4 July 1893, or a woman born between 5 July 1888 and 4 July 1898, qualifies for a grant of £15. People older than that do not qualify for a death grant.

The death grant must be claimed on a form (B.D.1) which you can get from a Department of Health and Social Security office or apply for on the back of the certificate of registration of deah (form B.D.8, given by the registrar for national insurance purposes). The completed application form for a death grant is returned to the local office of the Department. You must give particulars of the deceased on it and have to declare in what capacity you claim the grant. If you have not already sent in the certificate of registration of death (form B.D.8), evidence of death must accompany your completed application for a death grant. With the application form should also go the deceased's marriage certificate, if married; also the national insurance contribution card and any Department of Health and Social Security payment books not yet handed back. An undertaker's estimate or account may be required as evidence of the funeral. The grant is likely not to be paid unless claimed within six months of the death, so even if all the documents are not available, do not delay the claim. If a body has been given for medical research but the relatives are going to arrange the eventual funeral themselves, the death grant should be claimed now, not at the time of the funeral.

The grant will normally be paid within about ten days. It is usually an order which can be cashed at a post office.

If there is no funeral (for instance, after an accident when the body could not be recovered), the death grant is none the less paid to the executor or next of kin.

The death grant is not subject to estate duty. The amount of it must be deducted from the funeral expenses claimed from the deceased's estate.

There are reciprocal arrangements between this country and some overseas ones for payment of the death grant if a british citizen dies abroad. If you need to find out about claiming a death grant or a widow's benefit after someone has died abroad, write to the overseas branch of the Department of Health and Social Security in Newcastle upon Tyne NE98 1YX.

Widow's benefit

Widow's benefit is an omnibus term used by the Department of Health and Social Security for a number of payments for which a woman may become entitled following her husband's death.

A widow qualifies for benefit only if her husband's national insurance record satisfies the appropriate conditions. As against the qualifications for a death grant, her own contributions do not count. If his widow is to qualify for any benefits at all, the husband must have paid at least 156 contributions under the 1948 national insurance scheme (contributions credited during periods of illness or unemployment do not count). If he was insured under the pre-1948 pensions scheme, only 104 contributions may be required.

In order for his widow to get a full benefit, the husband must have paid, or had credited to him, an average of 50 contributions per insurance year between the date of his death, or his sixty-fifth birthday if he died after that age, and

– his sixteenth birthday if that was later than 5 July 1948
– *or* 5 July 1948 if he was then sixteen or over and started paying national insurance contributions on or after that date
– *or* the actual date on which he started to pay contributions if that was between 1936 and 5 July 1948
– *or* 1936 if he was paying into insurance before then.

If his average annual paid and credited contributions work out at between 13 and 49, his widow's benefit will be reduced. If his average works out at less than 13 a year, she will get nothing. A widow's own insurance record cannot be used instead of her late husband's to satisfy these conditions.

Only the lawful widow of an insured man can claim any widow's benefits on his death. If the marriage had been annulled or dissolved by divorce, the woman is not regarded

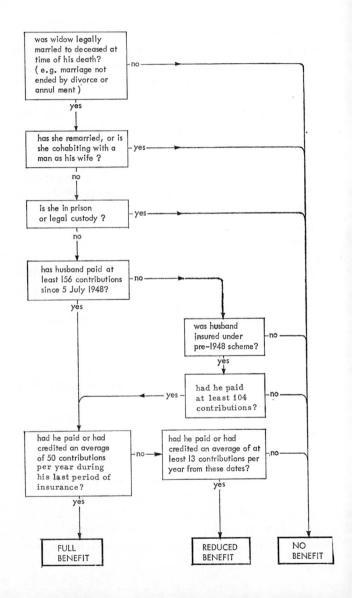

as his lawful widow. If a widow later marries, she loses her widow's benefit from her previous marriage. She will not be paid any benefit while she is in prison or other legal detention, or while cohabiting with a man as his wife.

A widow does not apply specifically for any one benefit but makes her claim on a detailed form (form B.W.1), available at any Department of Health and Social Security office or by applying for it on form B.D.8. On form B.W.1 she is asked to give particulars of herself and her husband and of any children under nineteen. She should send off the form as soon as possible and not later than three months after her husband's death in order not to lose any of the benefits. If she can send her marriage and birth certificates, too, it will speed things up.

About a fortnight after sending in the form, she will be informed in writing if her husband's contributions were insufficient for her to receive the full, or any, widow's benefit. If she disagrees with the decision, she has a right to appeal to the local insurance tribunal; she can discuss the procedure with her local citizens' advice bureau.

– widow's allowance

The widow of a man who had not yet retired (either because he was under 65 or had chosen to continue working after the as his lawful widow. If a widow later marries, she loses her age of 65 without drawing his pension) and whose national insurance record entitles her to benefits, receives an allowance of £8.40 a week for the first 26 weeks after her husband's death. She gets a book of weekly orders cashable at the post office she nominates on form B.W.1.

If a man had earned at least £450 gross in the last tax year before he died, his widow may be paid, on top of her £8.40 for the first 26 weeks after his death, a supplementary allowance related to her husband's earnings. This earnings-related allowance is based on the husband's average weekly pay and is limited to a maximum of £7 a week. A widow should be prepared to send details of her husband's recent employments and his last certificate of pay and tax deducted (given to employees after each tax year).

– widow's pension

After the first 26 weeks' allowance, a widow without children may receive a weekly pension, depending on age.

If the husband was 65 or more when they got married and he has died within a year of the marriage, his widow may not get a pension on his insurance record, or may get only a reduced one.

A widow under the age of 40 does not get a pension.

If a woman is between the ages of 40 and 50 when her husband dies, she gets a widow's pension calculated on a sliding scale according to her age when her husband dies, starting at £1.80 for a widow who is exactly 40 at the time, to £5.58 if she is 49.

A widow who is between the ages of 50 and 60 at the time of her husband's death receives a widow's pension of £6 a week.

However, if the husband did not contribute to the current national insurance scheme because he was over 65 on 5 July 1948, a widow's pension of between £1.08 and £3.60 a week may be payable, depending on her age when he died.

No widow's benefit is affected by any income the widow receives from any other source, such as from earnings or investments, but it is subject to income tax.

For the first 26 weeks after her husband's death, a widow need not pay national insurance contributions. After that period, she should make weekly contributions if she does not qualify for a widow's pension or a widowed mother's allowance. If she is getting an allowance or pension, she can choose whether to contribute or not. A widow who is getting a pension based on her husband's pre-1948 insurance must pay national insurance contributions. If a widow is employed, her employer may deduct graduated and industrial injury contributions from her pay.

– widow over sixty

If a woman is sixty or over at the time of her husband's death and they had both been drawing the retirement pension, she can ask on form B.D.8 for her retirement pension to be changed to the rate for a widow. A widow's pension is a basic £6 a week from the time of the husband's death, if his contributions qualify her for the full rate of pension, plus half his graduated pension additions. (2½p a week is added to retirement pensions for every unit – £7.50 for a man, £9 for a woman – of contributions paid since 1961 when the scheme began.) A widow over sixty cannot draw both a retirement and a widow's pension.

If a widow is already drawing a retirement pension on her own insurance and her husband's pension was at a higher rate than her own, her pension can be replaced by one based on his insurance record.

A woman who is not yet drawing a retirement pension when her husband dies may qualify for a widow's pension, even if she goes on working. Once she has retired, or reaches the age of 65, she inherits half her husband's graduated pension increases to add to her retirement pension as well as any of her own.

If her husband had not yet been getting a retirement pension, a widow receives the widow's allowance of £8.40 a week for the first 26 weeks after his death. If he had deferred his retirement, she gets an additional increase to her pension for the contributions he made between the ages of 65 and 70.

– war widow's pension

If her husband was, or had ever been, in the armed forces and his death could be attributed to his military service, the widow should write to the Department of Health and Social Security, Norcross, Blackpool, explaining the circumstances fully, and asking if she is entitled to a war widow's pension.

Widow with children

A widow gets an additional allowance from the date of her husband's death for each child under school-leaving age, or who is under nineteen and a full-time student or apprentice, or under sixteen and through prolonged illness or disability cannot work. The amounts are £2.95 a week for the first or only child, £2.05 for the second child, and £1.95 for each of all other children.

These payments are in addition to any family allowance she may be entitled to draw, so that she receives £2.95 per child. A widow can only claim the extra allowance for a child who was or would have been treated as part of her late husband's family, and normally only for a child living with her.

A widow with children who qualify receives a widowed mother's personal allowance of £6 for herself as well as the £2.95 for each child. A widow who is expecting a child by her late husband is paid the £6 personal allowance and after the child is born the additional £2.95 a week. A widow continues to get her personal allowance of £6 if any child past school-leaving age but not yet nineteen is still living with her; she does not get the £2.95 for the child. A widow who is under forty at the time when her children cease to qualify her for a widowed mother's allowance then gets nothing. A widow over 50 by that time continues to get a pension of £6 a week; if between 40 and 49, she gets from £1.80 to £5.58.

A divorced woman may on the death of her former husband

be paid at the rate of the £2.95 allowance for any child whom he had been maintaining. She can apply for this allowance on form C.S.1, which is available from any local office of the Department of Health and Social Security.

A widow with at least one child living with her under the age of sixteen or still at school is eligible for a family income supplement if she is working at least 30 hours a week and her normal gross weekly income from all sources is less than £18 a week, plus £2 for each additional child. The maximum supplement is £4 a week. (Increases are proposed from April 1972.) FIS 1 with a claim form is available from Social Security offices and post offices.

Industrial death benefits

If someone dies as the result of an accident at work or of one of the 40-odd causes classified as industrial diseases, his dependants can claim special benefits. Part of the normal national insurance contributions that employed people in most occupations pay is cover for industrial injury. There are no contribution requirements, and it does not matter how long the dead person had been employed in that occupation.

In the midst of the widow's claim form B.W.1 there is a question asking whether she claims that her husband's death was due to an industrial accident or prescribed industrial disease. If the answer is yes, she must send with the form the 10p death certificate for certain statutory purposes obtainable from the registrar, because this states the medical cause of death. She may have to provide further evidence, for example, that her husband had been receiving a disability pension, or the verdict of an inquest.

Any extra benefit due because the husband died as a result of an industrial injury or disease is paid only after the first 26 weeks. A widow under fifty then gets £1.80 a week. If she was over fifty at the time of her husband's death, the widow gets £6.55 a week. A widow who was pregnant at the time her husband died through an industrial accident or disease, or who is permanently unable to support herself, also gets £6.55 a week. So does a widow entitled to a widowed mother's allowance or who is over 40 when it ceases.

A widower who is permanently incapable of supporting himself and who was wholly or mainly maintained by his wife, receives a pension of £6.55 a week if she dies as a result of an industrial accident or disease. This is the only circumstance when a man receives a national insurance allowance on the death of his wife. He should make his claim on form B.I.200 available from the Department of Health and Social Security, with which he must send the 10p death certificate for statutory purposes and his marriage certificate.

Other dependants such as parents or other close relatives who had been supported by a man or woman who met an industrial death, can also claim on B.I.200 for a benefit, which will be either a weekly payment or a lump sum. The fact that one person is getting an industrial allowance after a death does not preclude another dependant getting one too.

Orphans

A person who takes into his family an orphaned child can claim a guardian's allowance of £2.95 a week, provided he contributes more than anyone else to the support of the orphan. Although the payment is called a guardian's allowance, it is not necessary to assume legal guardianship to qualify. Usually the allowance is paid only when both parents, whether natural or adoptive, are dead. Sometimes it is paid after the death of one of the parents; for example, if the other is untraceable or if a child had been adopted by a single person. No allowance can be paid unless one of the parents had paid, or been credited with, national insurance contributions. An allowance for a child cannot be awarded directly to the child, only to the person in whose family the child is included. Application for a guardian's allowance should be made on form B.G.1, which can be obtained from a Department of Health and Social Security office.

When there is no one to take charge of a child, the local authority's social services department should be told and will assume responsibility for the child. If at all possible, children of the same family are kept together.

APPLICATION FORMS FOR GRANTS, ALLOWANCES AND PENSIONS

B.D.8	from registrar, on back of certificate of registration/notification of death	to apply for form B.D.1 and for form B.W.1, or for an adjustment in retirement pension for a widow
B.D.1	from a Department of Health and Social Security office, or by sending form B.D.8	to apply for a death grant
B.W.1	from a Department of Health and Social Security office, or by sending form B.D.8	to claim widow's benefits
B.I.200	from a Department of Health and Social Security office	for widower and other dependants to apply for industrial death benefits
C.S.1	from a Department of Health and Social Security office	for a divorced woman to claim allowance for child(ren) on death of former husband
B.G.1	from a Department of Health and Social Security office	to apply for guardian's allowance for the support of an orphan
FIS.1	from a Department of Health and Social Security office or post offices	to apply for family income supplement
S.P.1 S.1	from post offices	to apply for supplementary pension or allowance

INDEX

allowances, *see* pensions
application forms
- for cemeteries, 45, 46, 48, 65, 78
- for crematoria, 50, 57, 65, 78
- for death certificates, 23, 25
- for national insurance benefits, 107
- for rates rebate, 91
see also forms
ashes, 53, 54
- disposal, 52, 54, 55, 56, 57, 65, 69, 70, 79
- sending abroad, 81

bearers, 59, 62, 69, 71
benefits, national insurance, 95 *et seq*
benevolent schemes, 94
bequeathing a body, 38 *et seq*
- claiming death grant, 40, 98
- cremation afterwards, 40, 51
bequest of eyes, 37, 38
birth certificate, 19, 22, 101
body
- before funeral, 9, 10, 12, 50, 51, 60, 61, 62, 64, 68, 78
- bequeathing, 38 *et seq*, 51, 98
- burial, 42 *et seq*
- cremation, 49 *et seq*
- disposal, 37 *et seq*
- embalming, 61, 62, 64, 78
- identifying, 11, 17, 18, 27, 69, 76
- laying out, 10, 61, 64
- responsibility for, 14, 27, 60, 85
- sending, 80, 81, 82, 83, 84, 85
book of remembrance
- in churches, 55
- in crematoria, 55, 56
brick grave, 47
British Humanist Association, 67
burial, 42 *et seq*
- abroad, 81, 82, 85
- of ashes, 54, 55, 57, 69, 79
- in cemeteries, 44 *et seq*, 78
- in churches, 44
- in churchyards, 42 *et seq*, 78
- in private ground, 48
- record of, 43, 47, 48, 73
- in the sea, 82
burial fees, 55, 71
- in cemeteries, 45, 46, 47

- in churchyards, 42, 43, 46
see also interment fees

cars, at funeral, 59, 62, 68, 79
- charge for extra mileage, 64
casket, 63
see also coffin
catafalque, 70
cause of death, 11, 12, 13, 14, 15, 16, 18, 19, 20, 21, 26, 27, 28, 39, 105
- ascertained before cremation, 50
- and hospital post mortem, 26
- found at inquest, 15
cemetery
- burial in, 44 *et seq*, 78, 79
- burial of ashes, 55, 69, 79
- forms required, 29, 45, 48, 65, 78
- memorials and flowers, 45, 72, 73, 74
- record of burials, 40, 47
certificates
- birth, 19, 22, 101
- of cause of death, 11 *et seq*
- for cremation, 17, 29, 50, 51, 54, 55, 57, 84, 87
- death, *see* death certificates
- disposal, *see* disposal certificate
- of embalming, 82
- from Home Office for cremation of body brought from abroad, 84
- after inquest, 17, 21
- of no liability to register, 83, 84
- marriage, 19, 98, 101, 106
- national savings, 23, 24, 35
- of notification of death, 22, 24, 107
- of pay and tax deducted, 102
- of registration of death, 22, 23, 24, 97, 98, 107
- for cremation of stillbirth, 52
- of stillbirth, 27, 28
Channel Islands, 81
chapel
- at undertaker's, 61, 62, 66
- in cemetery, 45, 66
- in crematorium, 53, 66, 67, 69, 70, 78
chapel of rest
- at undertaker's, 61, 62
- in crematorium, 53

chaplain, *see* clergy
children, 20, 23, 106
– and death grant, 97
– fees for burial or cremation, 47, 52
– and national insurance, 104 *et seq*
church
– body lying in overnight, 64, 68, 69
– book of remembrance, 55
– burial in, 44
– and disposal certificate, 29, 48
– fees, 44, 64, 65, 74
– and memorials, 44, 55, 73, 74
– service in, 42, 66, 69, 79
churchyards
– burial in, 42 *et seq*, 69, 78, 79
– burial of ashes, 55, 69, 79
– memorials, 73, 74
citizens' advice bureau, 91, 101
clergy, 64, 79
– fees, 64, 66
– roster at cemetery, 45
– roster at crematorium, 53
see also incumbent
clothes, disposing of, 92
coffin, 61 *et seq*
– for burial in the sea, 82
– and cremation, 53, 63
– sending abroad, 81, 82
columbarium, 55
committal
– room at crematorium, 53, 70
– words of, 66, 69, 70
complete/inclusive funeral, 62, 63, 64
consul, 82, 83
contributions, national insurance, 95 *et seq*
co-operative society funeral, 71
coroner, 12 *et seq*
– and burial in the sea, 82
– certifying cause of death, 11, 20, 21, 22, 28
– deaths reported to, 12, 13, 14, 19, 26, 27, 28, 76, 77
– and bequeathing body, 39
– and embalming, 62
– and eye bequests, 37
– giving authority to dispose of body, 17, 29, 48, 50, 51, 57, 65, 76
– and inquests, 14 *et seq*, 76

– and notice of intention to remove body, 81, 82, 84, 89
– notifying registrar, 12, 13, 14, 17, 21, 28, 76
– persons reporting death to, 12, 13, 19, 26, 27, 28, 51, 76, 77
– police taking evidence for, 11
coroner's
– certificate-for-cremation, 17, 29, 50, 51, 57
– certificate-after-inquest, 17, 21
– court, 15, 16, 17
– officer, 13, 14, 16
– order for burial, 17, 29, 48, 51
– summons, 15
costs, *see* fees
councils of social service, 94
cremation, 9, 49 *et seq*, 57, 76, 78, 79, 84
– of bequeathed body, 40, 51
– documents needed, 26, 30, 50, 51, 52, 57, 65, 76, 78, 83, 84
– and embalming, 62
– and jews, 67
– and roman catholics, 68
– service before, 53, 69, 70
Cremation Society, 49, 50
cremator, 53, 70
crematorium
– charges and conditions, 52, 53, 64, 65, 66, 67, 70, 78
– committal room, 53, 70
– disposal of ashes, 52, 54, 70, 79
– forms, 29, 49, 50, 52, 57, 65, 78, 84
– memorials and flowers, 54, 55, 56, 72, 73
– register of cremations, 54
Cruse clubs, 94

death, 9 *et seq*, 76
– abroad, 82, 83, 84, 98
– causes, 10, 11, 12, 13, 14, 15, 16, 19, 20, 26, 27, 50, 105
– in hospital, 26 *et seq*, 76
– presuming, 86
– registering, 17 *et seq*, 77
– as a result of war service, 13, 19, 86' 104
– on ship or aircraft, 85

see also medical cause of death
death certificates, 21, 22 *et seq*, 86
– confirming registration, notification of death, 22, 24, 97, 98, 107
– getting further copies, 24, 25
– for industrial death benefit, 24, 105, 106
– issued in another country, 83
– when sending body abroad, 82
– special, 23, 24
– standard, 22, 23, 24
– for statutory purposes, 23, 24
death grant, 24, 86, 90, 95 *et seq*, 107
– when body bequeathed, 40, 98
– when death abroad, 98
– and estate duty, 98
– and local authority, 86
deeds, grave, 46, 48, 65, 75, 80
denominations
– and burial, 44, 45, 67
– and cremation, 54, 68
– funerals, 66, 67, 68
Department of Health and Social Security
– and application forms, 107
– and death grant, 86, 97, 98
– and national insurance contributions, 95
– and national insurance benefits, 24, 95 *et seq*
– overseas branch, 98
– returning pension books to, 90
– and war pensioners, 86, 104
– and widow's benefit, 99 *et seq*
disposal, 29, 30, 37 *et seq*, 76, 78
– of ashes, 52, 54 *et seq*, 65, 69, 70, 79
– when body bequeathed, 40
– of stillborn child, 65
disposal certificate, 29 *et seq*, 40, 48, 50, 57, 60, 61, 62, 65, 76 *et seq*, 80, 81
– when body being taken out of country, 81, 83
divorced woman, 95, 99, 105, 107
doctor, 9 *et seq*, 76
– when body bequeathed, 38, 39, 40
– and bequest of eyes, 37
– certificate of cause of death, 11, 21, 27, 62, 76, 92

– and the coroner, 12, 13, 76
– and cremation, 9, 27, 50, 51, 52, 57, 62, 65, 76, 84
– fees, 51, 57, 65
– and stillbirth, 27, 28
documents
– for burial, 48
– for cremation, 57
– for registration, 21
– for removal of body to or from this country, 84
– of dead person, 90 *et seq*
see also forms
driving licence, 92

embalming, 61, 62, 64, 78, 81, 82
employers' pension schemes, 93
estate, administration of, 90 *et seq*
– paying funeral expenses, 60, 80
estate duty
– and death grant, 98
executor, 37, 38, 40, 41, 45, 46, 48, 49, 50, 57, 59, 60, 61, 69, 70, 71, 80, 81, 84, 90, 91, 95

faculty
– for burial of ashes in churchyard, 55
– for burial in churches, 44
– for erecting memorial over grave, 44, 74
– for memorial in churches, 44
– reserving grave, 43, 44, 48
family allowances, 22, 23, 104
family income supplement, 105
fees for
– average total for funeral, 65
– burial in cemeteries, 45, 46, 47
– burial in churchyards, 42, 43, 44, 67
– burial in the sea, 82
– certificate of no liability to register, 83, 84
– chapel of rest, 53, 64
– clergy at cremation, 53
– complete/inclusive funerals, 64
– copy of entry in burial register, 47, 48
– copy of entry in crematorium register, 54, 57

- cremation, 52, 53, 57, 71
- death certificate for friendly societies, 22, 23, 24
- death certificate for statutory purposes, 23, 24
- deed of grant for grave, 46
- disposal of ashes, 54, 55
- disposal of stillborn child, 65
- doctors completing forms B and C for cremation, 51, 57, 65, 71
- duplicate disposal certificate, 29
- embalming, 64
- entry in book of remembrance, 55
- exclusive right of burial in cemetery, 46, 47
- extra mileage or cars, 64
- faculty in churchyard, 43, 48
- flowers, 71, 73
- gravedigger in churchyard, 43, 66
- lawn graves, 46, 47
- laying out, 61, 64
- medical referee completing form F, 53, 57
- membership of Cremation Society, 49, 50
- memorials in churchyard or cemetery, 44, 46, 74
- memorials at crematoria, 55, 56
- miniature copy of book of remembrance, 56
- minimum service funeral, 64
- music at funeral, 42, 43, 44, 53, 64, 66
- notices in newspapers, 71, 72, 73
- permission to put up memorial on grave, 44, 46, 74
- plot in private gardens of remembrance, 56
- post mortem ordered by medical referee, 52
- removal of body, 61, 64
- removing and replacing headstone on grave, 43, 46
- reserving grave space in cemetery, 46
- search for entry in register of deaths, 25, 35
- sending coffin, 80, 81, 83
- services of British Humanist Association, 67
- services of National Secular Society, 67
- special death certificate, 23, 24
- standard death certificate, 22, 24
first offices, 61
flowers
- for funeral, 71, 72, 73, 79
- as memorial, 45, 56, 72, 73
forms
- of application for benefits, 107
- authorising removal of body from hospital, 61
- for bequeathing body, 38, 39, 40
- for bequest of eyes, 37
- BD1 (claiming death grant), 97, 107
- BD8 (applying to claim death benefits), 22, 23, 24, 97, 98, 101, 103, 107
- BG1 (application for guardian's allowance), 107
- BI200 (dependants' application for industrial death benefits), 106, 107
- BW1 (widow's application for benefits), 101, 103, 107
- for cemetery, 45, 47, 48, 65
- confirming arrangements with crematorium, 52, 57
- consenting to hospital post mortem, 26
- CS1 (application for child's special allowance), 105, 107
- expressing wish for cremation, 49
- FIS (family income supplement), 105, 107
- form 35 (declaration of stillbirth), 28
- form 104 (notice of intention to remove body), 81, 84
- required for cremation, 26, 40, 50 *et seq*, 57, 62, 65, 76, 78, 83, 84
- SP1, S1 (application for supplementary pension or allowance), 94, 107
friendly societies
- death certificate for claiming from, 22, 23, 24
- paying out on death, 60

funeral, 40, 59 *et seq*, 78, 79
– announcement in newspaper, 72, 79
– away, 80, 81
– after death abroad, 82 *et seq*
– costs, 60, 62 *et seq*, 85, 86
– and death grant, 95 *et seq*
– by hospital or local authority, 37, 85, 86
– pre-death arrangements, 80
– religious denominations, 66 *et seq*
– responsibility for, 18, 37, 40, 49, 52, 59, 60, 85, 86
– of serviceman, 85, 86
funeral directors, 59
see also undertakers
furniture, getting rid of, 90, 91

gardens of remembrance
– at crematoria, 54
– private, 56
General Register Office
– supplying copies of entry of death, 24, 25, 36, 83, 85
graduated pension scheme, 103
grants, 95 *et seq*
– after death of serviceman, 85, 86
see also pensions
grave
– in cemetery, 45, 46, 47, 48, 73, 78
– ceremony at, 66, 67, 69
– in churchyard, 43, 46, 48
– faculty, 43, 44, 48, 73, 78
– sizes and types, 47, 66, 78
grave deeds, 46, 48, 65, 74, 80
gravedigger, 43, 66, 71
guardian's allowance, 106, 107

handy, 61
hearse, 59, 61, 62, 64, 69, 80
Home Office, issuing certificate for cremation of body brought from abroad, 84
hospital
– arranging funeral, 37, 85
– and bequest of eyes, 37
– death in, 26 *et seq*, 76
– and flowers, 73
– post mortem, 26, 76
– removal of body from, 27, 61

Humanist Association, British, 67
hygienic treatment, *see* embalming

identification of body, 11, 18, 69, 76
– at hospital, 26
– through inquest, 15, 17
inclusive/complete funeral, 62, 63, 64
income tax, 90, 91
– and widow's benefits, 102
incumbent (vicar or rector)
– authority over churchyard, 42, 43, 44, 67, 73
– and burial of ashes, 69
– and burials in church, 44
see also clergy
industrial death benefits, 105 *et seq*
informant, 18 *et seq*, 30
inquest, 11, 13, 14 *et seq*, 76, 81
– coroner's authority to dispose of body after, 17, 29, 48, 57
– coroner's certificate-after-inquest, 17, 21
– jury, 16, 17
– verdict, 16, 17, 105
– witnesses, 11, 15, 16
inscriptions
– at crematoria, 55, 56
– on memorials, 44, 74
Inspector of Anatomy, HM
– and bequeathing a body, 38 *et seq*
insurance
– cancelling, 93
– death certificates for claiming, 23, 24
– for funeral, 60
– life policies, 19, 23 24 90, 93
see also national insurance
interment fees for
– ashes, 55
– brick grave in cemetery, 47
– faculty grave in churchyard, 43
– lawn grave in cemetery, 46, 47
– and non-ratepayers, 47
– private grave in cemetery, 46
– public grave in cemetery, 45
– reduced for children, 47

jews, funeral arrangements, 67, 68
jury at inquest, 16, 17

last offices, 61
lawn grave, 46, 47
– headstone, 46, 74
laying out, 9, 10, 61, 64
letters of administration, 90
– and death certificate, 22
library books, records, tickets, 93
local authority
– caring for orphans, 107
– cemeteries, 45 *et seq*
– crematoria, 53, 56
– and death grant, 86
– funerals, 37, 85, 86
– refuse department, 91
London Transport, refunds, 92

mail, dealing with deceased's, 92
marriage certificate, 19, 98, 101, 106
medical card, 21, 90
medical cause of death, *see* cause of death
medical certificate
– for cremation of stillbirth, 52
– when body bequeathed, 38, 39, 40
– of cause of death, 11 *et seq*, 62, 76
medical officer of health, authority to dispose of body, 30
medical referee of crematorium, 51, 52, 66, 84
– and cremation of body from abroad, 84
– signing form F (authority to cremate), 51, 52, 53, 57
medical research, *see* bequeathing body
medical school
– arrangements for bequeathing body to, 38 *et seq*
– claiming death grant, 40
– cremation of bodies, 51
memorial service, 72, 79
memorials, 40, 73, 74, 79
– in cemeteries, 45, 46, 73, 74
– in church, 44
– in churchyard, 43, 44, 55
– at crematoria, 55, 56
mileage limits, 62, 64, 80
minimum funeral service scheme, 64

Ministry of Defence
– arranging funeral of serviceman, 85
monumental stone masons, 74
mortgage, continuing payments, 91
mortuary, 11, 14, 62
– at hospital, 26, 27
– undertaker fetching body, 60, 64
mother
– registering stillbirth, 27, 28
– widowed, *see* widowed mother
mourners, 68, 69, 70, 79
murder, manslaughter, 15
music
– in church, 42, 43
– in crematorium chapel, 53
– fees for, 42, 64, 66

nameplate on coffin, 63
National Association of Funeral Directors, 59
– minimum funeral service scheme, 64
national health service
– medical card, 21, 90
– number, 20
– providing shroud, 26
national insurance benefits, 95 *et seq*
– application forms for claiming, 107
National Insurance Acts, death certificate for claiming under, 23, 24
national savings certificates, 23, 24, 35
National Secular Society, 67
Northern Ireland
– address of General Register Office, 25
– bringing body from England or Wales, 81
– death certificates, 22, 24, 25, 83
– doctor seeing deceased before death, 12
– search fee, 25
notice to informant, 18, 21, 76
notices in newspapers, 71, 72, 73, 92
notification of death, certificate of, 22, 24, 107
nurse, laying out body, 10, 61
NYD ('not yet dead') funeral arrangements, 80

officer's war service pension, 90
order book for pensions or allowances, 22, 90, 98
order for burial, coroner's, 17, 29, 48,
   51
organ, *see* music
organisations
– to help those alone, 94
– running benevolent schemes, 94
orphans, 106, 107
pall
– bearers, 69
– on coffin, 63, 69
parish
– boundaries, 42
– churchyards, 42, 43
– regulations, 44, 67
parishioners, right of burial, 42
parochial church council, 42, 43
passport, returning, 92
pensions, 95 *et seq*
– claiming unpaid amounts, 89
– employers' schemes, 24, 93
– graduated, 103
– order book, 22, 90, 98
– list of application forms for, 107
– supplementary, 93, 94
– based on war service, 22, 86, 90
– war widow's, 104
– widow's, 102 *et seq*
   see also grants, national insurance
personal representative, duties of, 90
police, 10, 11, 15
– in charge of body, 18, 85
– and dead person's belongings, 11
– and inquests, 15
– reporting death to coroner, 13
– and suspicious death, 10, 11, 76
– telling next of kin, 14, 26, 76
– and unidentified persons, 11
possessions, 11, 90 *et seq*
– collecting from hospital, 26, 76
post office savings, 23, 24, 35
post mortem, 13, 14, 29, 39, 57, 76
– and body after, 14, 60, 77
– by hospital, 26
– ordered by coroner, 14, 81
– ordered by medical referee, 51, 52
– staining, 10

pre-1948 pensions scheme, 99, 103
pre-death arrangements, 80
pregnant widow, 104, 106
premium savings bonds, 23, 24, 35
preservative treatment, *see* embalming
presuming death, 86
private funeral, 72
private or purchased grave, 46, 47, 78
– deed of grant, 46
– and memorials, 73, 74
probate, 90
– and death certificates, 21, 22, 24
– and deceased's names, 19
– and paying undertaker, 71
property
– disposing of, 90 *et seq*
– police taking, 11

rail charges for coffin, 80
rates rebate, 91
record
– of graves in cemetery, 40, 47
– of graves in churchyards, 43
– of national insurance contributions,
   95
records, returning to library, 93
rector, *see* incumbent
refrigeration, 62
refunds, 92, 93
– of income tax, 91
register of burials, 43, 47, 48, 73
register of cremations, 54, 57
register of deaths
– copies of entry, 21 *et seq*
– entry in, 19 *et seq*
registering death, 11, 17 *et seq*, 77
– abroad, 82, 83
– after death in hospital, 27
– after inquest, 17
– after stillbirth, 27, 28
– when body bequeathed, 39, 40
– certificates after, *see* death certificates
– documents needed, 21
registrar of births and deaths
– and application forms for death
   certificates, 24, 25
– contacting next of kin, 13, 14

– giving copies of entry in register of deaths, 21 *et seq*, 77
see also death certificates
– and informant, 18, 21, 27
– issuing certificate of no liability to register, 83, 84
– issuing disposal certificate, 29, 30, 48, 57, 77, 81
– and medical certificate of cause of death, 12, 18, 19, 21
– notified by coroner, 12, 13, 14, 17, 21, 28, 76
– and part C of disposal certificate, 29, 48, 57
– registering death, 19 *et seq*
– reporting death to coroner, 13, 19, 77
– reporting death to medical officer of health, 29
– requiring evidence of death abroad, 83
– and stillbirths, 28
– supplying form 104, 81, 84
– taking deceased's medical card and pension book, 21, 90
– where to find, 17, 18, 25
– who gives information to, 18, 27, 77
registrar, diocesan, 43
registrar general
– and Scotland, 36
– authority to correct entry in register of deaths, 21
– preparation of population statistics, 20
religious service, *see* service
rent, continuing payments, 91
reposing room, *see* chapel of rest
retirement pension, 103
rigor mortis, 10
robe, 61, 64
roman catholic, funeral arrangements, 68
– coffin in church overnight, 68, 69
Royal National Institute for the Blind, 37

scattering of ashes, 54, 55, 70, 79

Scotland, 31 *et seq*, 88, 89
– bequeathing body, 38
– bequest of eyes, 37
– body brought from England or Wales, 81
– bringing body from abroad, 89
– burial, 88
– certificate of registration, 34, 35
– cremation, 88
– death certificates, 35, 36, 83
– disposal, 88
– General Register Office, 36
– medical certificate of cause of death, 33, 34
– procurator fiscal, 31 *et seq*, 89
– registering death, 33, 34
– Scottish Home and Health Department, 38, 89
– Scottish National Federation for the Welfare of the Blind, 37
– search fees, 35
– sending body abroad, 88, 89
– stillbirths, 34
Secular Society, National, 67
service, religious, 40, 66, 79
– burial or cremation without, 43, 53, 66, 67, 69, 70
– at cemeteries, 45, 66, 67
– in church, 42, 66, 69
– at cremation, 53, 66, 69, 70
– at undertaker's, 61
serviceman (member of armed forces)
– funeral, 85, 86
– war service pension, 22, 86, 90
– widow's benefit, 104
shell, 61
shroud, 26, 61, 64
slumber room, *see* chapel of rest
Social Security, *see* Department of Health and
solicitor
– advising about housing, 91
– at inquest, 16
special allowance, child's, 105
special death certificate, 23, 24
standard death certificate, 22, 23, 24, 82
state death grant, *see* death grant
stillbirths, 27, 28, 52, 65, 97

subscriptions, cancelling, 93
suicides, 13
supplementary allowance, 94
– earnings-related, widow's, 103
Supplementary Benefits Commission, 86
supplementary pension, 94
synagogues, 67, 68

telephone, notifying area manager, 93
tickets
– claiming refund on, 92
– returning library, 93
tips, 71
trustee savings bank, 23, 24

undertakers, 14, 42, 59 *et seq*, 77, 78, 79
– advising about memorials, 74
– arranging removal of body, 9, 39, 40, 60, 61, 64, 77, 80, 81, 82, 83
– charges and payments, 62, 63, 64, 65, 66, 70, 71, 79, 98
– and cremation, 50, 57, 70, 78, 84
– disposal of stillborn child, 65
– and embalming, 61, 62, 78
– and flowers, 73
– and gravedigger, 42, 66
– and newspaper notices, 71, 72, 79
– laying out body, 9, 10, 61, 64
– local authority funerals, 85
– and pre-death arrangements, 80
– premises, 61, 62, 64, 66
urns

– for ashes, 55, 70
– for flowers on graves, 73
vault, 47
verdict, at inquest, 16, 17, 105
vicar, *see* incumbent

war service
– death as result of, 13, 19, 86, 104
– pension or allowance, 22, 86, 90
war widow's pension, 104
widow
– and benevolent schemes, 94
– claiming benefits, 99 *et seq*, 107
– and Cruse clubs, 94
– if income reduced below guaranteed minimum, 93, 94
– paying national insurance contributions, 102, 103
– pregnant when husband died, 104, 106
– and rates rebate, 90
widow's benefit, 24, 99 *et seq*
– after death abroad, 98
– allowance (first 26 weeks), 101, 102
– applying for, 24, 101, 107
– industrial death, 105
– if over sixty, 103
– pension (after 26 weeks), 102
– qualifications, 99
widowed mother, 104, 105, 106
widower, 106
– industrial death benefit, 106
will, 90
– and disposal instructions, 37
witnesses at inquest, 11, 15, 16

WILLS AND PROBATE   60p
This is a book about wills and how to make them, and about the
administration of an estate undertaken by executors without the help
of a solicitor. A special section deals with intestacy and explains the
difficulties which can arise when there is no will.

Wills and probate follows Matthew Seaton step by step through the
tasks of an executor concerned with a straightforward will. Reading
the will, the valuation of the estate, payment of estate duty, the
steps involved in obtaining probate, the distribution of the estate in
accordance with the will, are all covered. Matthew also carries out
the transfer of property to the new owner. *Wills and probate* explains
clearly the procedures involved at every stage. The book also shows
how to make a will – prepare it, sign it and have it witeussed.

AILMENTS AND REMEDIES   60p
This Consumer Publication advocates intelligent self-medication and
provides a plain and simple guide to carrying it out. Common minor
ailments are discussed in a calm, authoritative way and the remedies are
given; where relevant, the (much cheaper) standard preparations are
suggested.

ARRANGEMENTS FOR OLD AGE   60p
is a book for those who are already old, for those who are approach-
ing old age, and for those who are concerned about the needs and
care of an older relative or friend.

It explains the local statutory and voluntary provisions for the
welfare of old people, and suggests how problems such as shortage
of money, ill health, lack of occupation, housing and the need for
residential care might be solved. Income tax and pension arrangements for people of retirement age are described.

HEALTH FOR OLD AGE   60p
is written in layman's language to help older people to understand
and cope with the difficulties and illnesses that may arise with
advancing years. The book advises generally on maintaining health
and talks sensibly about such afflictions as arthritis, thrombosis,
constipation, failing sight and hearing, heart failure. Symptoms to
report to the doctor are discussed, and remedies available. There is a
chapter on death and bereavement.

THE LEGAL SIDE OF BUYING A HOUSE £1

This book explains, step by step, the procedure on the typical transfer of a house in England or Wales (but *not* Scotland), which is wholly occupied by the seller and has a registered title.

The legal side of buying a house also deals with the somewhat less complicated business of the legal side of selling a house.

BUYING SECONDHAND 60p

tells you about buying in auction rooms, from dealers, shops and markets and through For Sale advertisements, and discusses in general terms the legal aspects of buying secondhand, commenting on price levels and guarantees. It gives you advice about buying secondhand furniture, photographic equipment, household appliances, cars, and so on, and has some useful hints, too, on selling secondhand.

THE LAW FOR CONSUMERS 60p

Written entirely in layman's language it extracts from the complexity of the law the essence of that part which has an impact on the consumer and explains how he can enforce his rights.

THE LAW FOR MOTORISTS 60p

Most people are hazy about the law for motorists, although at any time on any journey they may find themselves face to face with some aspect of it. *The law for motorists* is written in non-technical language and enables the motorist to find out how the law affects him.

OWNING A CAR 75p

For the ignorant car owner/driver, this book explains in non-technical language exactly what is involved in buying a car (new or used), the responsibilities of ownership, including repairs and maintenance, and suggests action even the most uninitiated motorist can take if his car breaks down. The book also includes information about learning to drive, what to do after an accident, laying up the car, towing, and the MoT test. It ends with a general assessment of the cost of owning a car.

CONSUMER'S CAR GLOSSARY 40p

Cars have their own language – the language of the car enthusiast, the mechanic, the car salesman and the motoring correspondent. The *Consumer's car glossary* is a dictionary of the terms of this language.

THE TRAVELLING CONSUMER 40p

provides much useful information and advice on how to deal with the problems and situations that may arise when planning a journey, during your holiday, and after it.

INFERTILITY 60p

sets out what can and should happen in the systematic investigation of childlessness and puts into perspective the physical factors associated with infertility.

PREGNANCY MONTH BY MONTH 60p

goes step by step through what should happen when having a baby. Some of the things that can go wrong during pregnancy and child-birth are discussed, and what can be done about them.

HOW TO ADOPT 60p

describes the process of adoption step by step. Aspects discussed in detail are eligibility to adopt, how to find a child, fostering, the child and his background, the legal situation, the effect of the adoption order – and after.

CARING FOR TEETH 60p

tells people how to look after their teeth. There is advice about diet and oral hygiene, and a section about the profession describes the general dental service, private dentistry and ancillary help. Other chapters describe dental and periodontal diseases and the treatment available, false teeth and how to look after them, and what to do and where to go in an emergency. Fees and charges for treatment and appliances are dealt with.

FORMAL ASPECTS OF MARRIAGE 60p

first describes in some detail the various procedures for getting married in England and Wales, in Scotland and in Northern Ireland, dealing with statutory requirements rather than wedding etiquette. The rest of the book is concerned with the status of being married, explaining about legal rights and duties, ownership of property, tax, national insurance, parental responsibilities.

GETTING A DIVORCE   60p
gives a step-by-step account of the procedure for getting a divorce in
England or Wales under the divorce law since 1971. It explains what has
to happen before and at the hearing in court, and when making
arrangements afterwards.

EXTENDING YOUR HOUSE   £1
tells in detail what has to be done at the various stages of a house
extension scheme. It is not a do-it-yourself manual but describes the
role of the architect or other consultant and the builder, and explains
about planning permission and the building regulations in England and
Wales.

TREATMENT AND CARE IN MENTAL ILLNESS   75p
deals briefly with the illnesses concerned and describes the help available
from the local authority and voluntary organisations. It explains the
medical treatment a mentally ill person receives as an outpatient or an
inpatient, and deals with community care and aftercare.

CONSUMER PUBLICATIONS are available from
Consumers' Association, Caxton Hill, Hertford,
post free, or through booksellers.